To: _Linda Jones_ 2004

From: _____

God longs for you to discover the life
he created you to live—here on earth,
and forever in eternity!
<small>RICK WARREN</small>

Requests for information should be addressed to:
Inspirio, The gift group of Zondervan
Grand Rapids, Michigan 49530
http://www.inspiriogifts.com

Associate Editor: Janice Jacobson
Compiler: Molly C. Detweiler
Designer: Sherri L. Hoffman
Design Manager: Amy Wenger
Illustrator: Michael Halbert © 2002

Printed in China

03 04 05/HK/ 3 2

DAILY
INSPIRATION
FOR
THE
PURPOSE-
DRIVEN®
Life

CONTENTS

—— ✍ ——

THE FIVE PURPOSES OF A PURPOSE-DRIVEN LIFE

You were made to live a purpose-driven life! The five purposes of your life are:

1. **WORSHIP: You were planned for God's pleasure!**
   After all this, there is only one thing to say: Have reverence for God, and obey his commands, because this is all that we were created for. ECCLESIASTES 12:13 TEV

2. **FELLOWSHIP: You were formed for a family!**
   It was a happy day for him when he gave us our new lives, through the truth of his Word, and we became, as it were, the first children in his new family. JAMES 1:18 LB

3. **DISCIPLESHIP: You were created to become like Christ!**
   God knew what he was doing from the very beginning. He decided from the outset to shape the lives of those who love him along the same lines as the life of his Son. The Son stands first in the line of humanity restored. We see the original and intended shape of our lives in him. ROMANS 8:29 THE MESSAGE

4. **MINISTRY: You were shaped for serving God!**
We are God's workmanship, created in Christ Jesus to do good works, which God prepared in advance for us to do.

Ephesians 2:10 NIV

5. **EVANGELISM: You were made for a mission!**
Jesus said, "Go and make disciples of all nations, baptizing them in the name of the Father and of the Son and of the Holy Spirit, and teaching them to obey everything I have commanded you. And surely I am with you always, to the very end of the age."

Matthew 28:19–20 NIV

WHAT ON EARTH
AM I HERE FOR?

———— ✍ ————

A life devoted to things is a dead life, a stump;
a God-shaped life is a flourishing tree.
PROVERBS 11:28 THE MESSAGE

———

Blessed are those who trust in the Lord and have
made the Lord their hope and confidence. They
are like trees planted along the riverbank, with
roots that reach deep into the water. Such trees
are not bothered by the heat or worried by long
months of drought. Their leaves stay green, and
they go right on producing delicious fruit.
JEREMIAH 17:7–8 NLT

———

It All Starts with God

For everything, absolutely everything, above and below, visible and invisible, rank after rank of angels—everything got started in him and finds its purpose in him.

COLOSSIANS 1:16 THE MESSAGE

It is God who directs the lives of his creatures;
everyone's life is in his power.

JOB 12:10 GNT

———

Obsession with self in these matters is a dead
end; attention to God leads us out into the open,
into a spacious, free life.

—ROMANS 8:6 THE MESSAGE

———

Jesus said, "Self-help is no help at all. Self-
sacrifice is the way, my way, to finding yourself,
your true self."

MATTHEW 16:25 THE MESSAGE

———

God's wisdom is something mysterious that goes deep into the interior of his purposes. You don't find it lying around on the surface. It's not the latest message, but more like the oldest—what God determined as the way to bring out his best in us, long before we ever arrived on the scene.

1 CORINTHIANS 2:7 THE MESSAGE

———

It's in Christ that we find out who we are and what we are living for. Long before we first heard of Christ and got our hopes up, he had his eye on us, had designs on us for glorious living, part of the overall purpose he is working out in everything and everyone.

EPHESIANS 1:11 THE MESSAGE

———

REFLECTIONS

_____

_____

_____

_____

_____

_____

_____

_____

_____

_____

_____

_____

_____

_____

_____

_____

_____

_____

_____

_____

_____

You are Not an Accident

I am your Creator.
You were in my care even before you were born.
ISAIAH 44:2 CEV

The LORD will fulfill his purpose for me.

PSALM 138:8 NIV

———

You know me inside and out,
   you know every bone in my body;
You know exactly how I was made, bit by bit,
   how I was sculpted from nothing into
      something.

PSALM 139:15 THE MESSAGE

———

You saw me before I was born and scheduled
each day of my life before I began to breathe.
Every day was recorded in your Book!

PSALM 139:16 LB

———

From one man God made every nation of men, that they should inhabit the whole earth; and he determined the times set for them and the exact places where they should live.

ACTS 17:26 NIV

Long before he laid down earth's foundations, he had us in mind, had settled on us as the focus of his love, to be made whole and holy by his love.

EPHESIANS 1:4 THE MESSAGE

God decided to give us life through the word of truth so we might be the most important of all the things he made.

JAMES 1:18 NCV

God formed the earth and made it.
He set it up.
He did not create it to be empty
    but formed it to be inhabited.

ISAIAH 45:18 GWT

———

God is love.

1 JOHN 4:8 NIV

———

"I have carried you since you were born;
    I have taken care of you from your birth.
Even when you are old, I will be the same.
    Even when your hair has turned gray,
        I will take care of you.
I made you and will take care of you,"
    says the LORD.

ISAIAH 46:3–4 NCV

———

The only accurate way to understand
ourselves is by what God is and by
what he does for us.

ROMANS 12:3 THE MESSAGE

———

REFLECTIONS

_____

_____

_____

_____

_____

_____

_____

_____

_____

_____

_____

_____

_____

_____

_____

_____

_____

_____

What Drives Your Life?

Everyone's life is driven by something; many are driven by things like guilt, resentment, anger, fear, materialism, and the need for approval.

To worry yourself to death with resentment would be a foolish, senseless thing to do.

JOB 5:2 TEV

I observed that the basic motive for success is the driving force of envy and jealousy!

ECCLESIASTES 4:4 LB

A pretentious, showy life is an empty life;
   a plain and simple life is a full life.

PROVERBS 13:7 THE MESSAGE

There are other forces that can drive your life but all lead to the same dead end: unused potential, unnecessary stress, and an unfulfilled life.

I have labored to no purpose;
   I have spent my strength in vain and for
      nothing.

ISAIAH 49:4 NIV

My life drags by—day after hopeless day.

JOB 7:6 LB

I give up; I am tired of living.
   Leave me alone. My life makes no sense.

JOB 7:16 TEV

You will be a restless wanderer on the earth.
GENESIS 4:12 NIV

The Bible has a remedy.

Don't live carelessly, unthinkingly. Make sure you
understand what the Master wants.

EPHESIANS 5:17 THE MESSAGE

Reflect on what I am saying [about serving the
Lord], for the Lord will give you insight into all
this.

2 TIMOTHY 2:7 NIV

Jesus said, "I am the way and the truth and the
life. No one comes to the Father except through
me."

JOHN 14:6 NIV

The Benefits of Purpose-Driven Living

Knowing your purpose gives your life meaning, simplicity, focus and motivation. It also prepares you for eternity.

What happiness for those whose guilt has been forgiven! What joys when sins are covered over! What relief for those who have confessed their sins and God has cleared their record.

PSALM 32:1 LB

Well-formed love banishes fear. Since fear is crippling, a fearful life—fear of death, fear of judgment—is one not yet fully formed in love.

1 JOHN 4:18 THE MESSAGE

"I know what I am planning for you," says the Lord. "I have good plans for you, not plans to hurt you. I will give you hope and a good future."

JEREMIAH 29:11 NCV

Glory be to God, who by his mighty power at work within us is able to do far more than we would ever dare to ask or even dream of—infinitely beyond our highest prayers, desires, thoughts, or hopes.

EPHESIANS 3:20 LB

You, LORD, give perfect peace
to those who keep their purpose firm
and put their trust in you.

ISAIAH 26:3 TEV

I am focusing all my energies on this one thing: Forgetting the past and looking forward to what lies ahead, I strain to reach the end of the race and receive the prize for which God, through Christ Jesus, is calling us up to heaven.

PHILIPPIANS 3:13 NLT

Let's keep focused on that goal, those of us who want everything God has for us. If any of you have something else in mind, something less than total commitment, God will clear your blurred vision—you'll see it yet!

PHILIPPIANS 3:15 THE MESSAGE

REFLECTIONS

_____

_____

_____

_____

_____

_____

_____

_____

_____

_____

_____

_____

_____

_____

_____

_____

_____

_____

_____

Made to Last Forever

God has planted eternity in the human heart.
ECCLESIASTES 3:11 NLT

God designed you, in his image, to live for eternity.

When this tent we live in—our body here on earth—is torn down, God will have a house in heaven for us to live in, a home he himself has made, which will last forever.

2 CORINTHIANS 5:1 TEV

When you fully comprehend that there is more to life than just here and now, you will begin to live differently. You will start *living in the light of eternity*.

I was circumcised when I was eight days old, having been born into a pure-blooded Jewish family that is a branch of the tribe of Benjamin. So I am a real Jew if there ever was one! What's more, I was a member of the Pharisees, who demand the strictest obedience to the Jewish law. And zealous? Yes, in fact, I harshly persecuted the church. And I obeyed the Jewish law so carefully that I was never accused of any fault. I once thought all these things were so very important, but now I consider them worthless because of what Christ has done. Yes, everything else is worthless when compared with the priceless gain of knowing Christ Jesus my Lord.

PHILIPPIANS 3:5–8 NLT

This world is not our home; we are looking forward to our everlasting home in heaven.

HEBREWS 13:14 LB

———

This world is fading away, along with everything it craves. But if you do the will of God, you will live forever.

1 JOHN 2:17 NLT

———

God's plans endure forever;
  his purposes last eternally.

PSALM 33:11 TEV

———

Every moment we spend in these earthly bodies is time spent away from our eternal home in heaven with Jesus.

2 CORINTHIANS 5:6 LB

———

What is it going to be like in eternity with God? Frankly, the capacity of our brains cannot handle the wonder and greatness of heaven.

No mere man has ever seen, heard or even imagined what wonderful things God has ready for those who love the Lord.

1 Corinthians 2:9 LB

———

Jesus will say, "Come, you who are blessed by my Father; take your inheritance, the kingdom prepared for you since the creation of the world."

Matthew 25:34 NIV

———

REFLECTIONS

_____

_____

_____

_____

_____

_____

_____

_____

_____

_____

_____

_____

_____

_____

_____

_____

_____

_____

_____

_____

_____

Seeing Life from God's View

Do not conform yourselves to the standards of
this world, but let God transform you inwardly by
a complete change of your mind. Then you will be
able to know the will of God.

— ROMANS 12:2 TEV

What is your life?

JAMES 4:14 NIV

The Bible offers three metaphors that teach us God's view of life:

1. Life on earth is a test. The good news is that God wants you to pass the tests of life.

God keeps his promise, and he will not allow you to be tested beyond your power to remain firm; at the time you are put to the test, he will give you the strength to endure it, and so provide you with a way out.

1 CORINTHIANS 10:13 TEV

Blessed are those who endure when they are tested. When they pass the test, they will receive the crown of life that God has promised to those who love him.

JAMES 1:12 GWT

God withdrew from Hezekiah in order to test him and to see what was really in his heart.

2 CHRONICLES 32:31 NLT

2. Life on earth is a trust. We never really own
anything during our brief stay on earth. God
just loans *the earth to us while we're here.*

What do you have that God hasn't given you? And
if all you have is from God, why boast as though
you have accomplished something on your own?

1 CORINTHIANS 4:7 NLT

The world and all that is in it belong to the LORD;
the earth and all who live on it are his.

PSALM 24:1 TEV

God blessed [Adam and Eve], and said, "Have
many children, so that your descendants will live
all over the earth and bring it under control. I am
putting you in charge."

GENESIS 1:28 TEV

Those who are trusted with something valuable
must show they are worthy of that trust.

1 CORINTHIANS 4:2 NCV

If you are untrustworthy about worldly wealth,
who will trust you with the true riches of heaven?

LUKE 16:11 NLT

Jesus said, "From everyone who has been given
much, much will be demanded; and from the one
who has been entrusted with much, much more
will be asked."

LUKE 12:48 NIV

Unless you are faithful in small matters, you won't
be faithful in large ones.

LUKE 16:10 NLT

**If you treat everything as a *trust*, God
promises three rewards in eternity:
affirmation, *promotion*, and *celebration*.**

Well done, good and faithful servant! You have
been faithful with a few things; I will put you in
charge of many things. Come and share your
master's happiness.

MATTHEW 25:21 NIV

REFLECTIONS

_____

_____

_____

_____

_____

_____

_____

_____

_____

_____

_____

_____

_____

_____

_____

_____

_____

_____

_____

_____

_____

Life is a Temporary Assignment

———— ✍ ————

LORD, remind me how brief my time on earth
  will be.
Remind me that my days are numbered,
and that my life is fleeing away.
PSALM 39:4 NLT

———

3. The last metaphor of life is that it is a temporary assignment.

For we were born but yesterday and know so littleOur days on earth are as transient as a shadow.

JOB 8:9 NLT

———

I am here on earth for just a little while.

PSALM 119:19 TEV

———

I am but a foreigner here on earth.

PSALM 119:19 NLT

———

If you call God your Father, live your time as temporary residents on earth.

1 PETER 1:17 GWT

———

There are many whose conduct shows they are really enemies of the cross of Christ. . . . All they think about is this life here on earth. But we are citizens of heaven, where the Lord Jesus Christ lives.

PHILIPPIANS 3:18–20 NLT

———

Lord, help me to realize how brief my time on earth will be. Help me to know that I am here for but a moment more.

PSALM 39:4 LB

Friends, this world is not your home, so don't make yourselves cozy in it. Don't indulge your ego at the expense of your soul.

1 PETER 2:11 THE MESSAGE

The things we see now are here today, gone tomorrow. But the things we can't see now will last forever.

2 CORINTHIANS 4:18 THE MESSAGE

Realizing that life on earth is just a temporary assignment should radically alter your values.

Those in frequent contact with the things of the world should make good use of them without becoming attached to them, for this world and all it contains will pass away.

1 CORINTHIANS 7:31 NLT

We fix our eyes not on what is seen, but on what is unseen. For what is seen is temporary, but what is unseen is eternal.

2 CORINTHIANS 4:18 NIV

———

You're cheating on God. If all you want is your own way, flirting with the world every chance you get, you end up enemies of God and his way.

JAMES 4:4 THE MESSAGE

———

In God's eyes, the greatest heroes of the faith are not those who achieve prosperity, success, and power in this life, but those who treat this life as a temporary assignment and serve faithfully, expecting their promised reward in eternity.

All these [heroes of the faith] died in faith. They did not get the things that God promised his people. But they saw them coming far in the future and were glad. They said they were like visitors and strangers on earth. . . . they were waiting for a better country—a heavenly country. So God is not ashamed to be called their God, because he has prepared a city for them.

HEBREWS 11:13, 16 NCV

———

We are Christ's ambassadors.

2 CORINTHIANS 5:20 NLT

———

REFLECTIONS

_____

_____

_____

_____

_____

_____

_____

_____

_____

_____

_____

_____

_____

_____

_____

_____

_____

_____

_____

_____

DAILY INSPIRATION FOR THE PURPOSE-DRIVEN LIFE

The Reason for Everything

———— 🐿 ————

Everything comes from God alone. Everything
lives by his power, and everything is for his glory.

ROMANS 11:36 LB

———

The LORD has made everything for his own
    purposes.
                    PROVERBS 16:4 NLT

Everything created by God reflects his glory
in some way.

The heavens declare the glory of God.
                    PSALM 19:1 NIV

The city [to come] does not need the sun or the
moon to shine on it, for the glory of God gives it
light.
                    REVELATION 21:23 NIV

You are worth, O Lord our God,
    to receive glory and honor and power.
For you created everything.
                    REVELATION 4:11 NLT

"They are my own people,
    and I created them to bring me glory,"
        says the Lord.
                    ISAIAH 43:7 TEV

Arise, shine, for your light has come,
    and the glory of the LORD rises upon you.
                    ISAIAH 60:1 NIV

God's glory is best seen in Jesus Christ.

The Son is the radiance of God's glory.

HEBREWS 1:3 NIV

The Word became human and lived among us. We saw his glory. It was the glory that the Father shares with his only Son, a glory full of kindness and truth.

JOHN 1:14 GWT

Jesus prayed to his Father, "I brought glory to you here on earth by doing everything you told me to do."

JOHN 17:4 NLT

Jesus prayed, "My soul has become troubled; and what shall I say, 'Father, save Me from this hour'? But for this purpose I came to this hour. Father, glorify Thy name."

JOHN 12:27–28 NASB

We bring God glory by worshiping him, loving other believers, becoming like Christ, serving others with our gifts, and telling others about him.

Use your whole body as a tool to do what is right for the glory of God.

ROMANS 6:13 NLT

———

Our love for each other proves that we have gone from death to life.

1 JOHN 3:14 CEV

———

Accept each other just as Christ has accepted you; then God will be glorified.

ROMANS 15:7 NLT

———

Jesus said, "As I have loved you, so you must love one another. By this all men will know that you are my disciples, if you love one another."

JOHN 13:34–35 NIV

———

As the Spirit of the Lord works within us, we become more and more like Christ and reflect his glory even more.

2 Corinthians 3:18 NLT

———

May you always be filled with the fruit of your salvation—those good things that are produced in your life by Jesus Christ—for this will bring much glory and praise to God.

Philippians 1:11 NLT

———

God has given gifts to each of you from his great variety of spiritual gifts. Manage them well so that God's generosity can flow through you. Are you called to be a speaker? Then speak as though God himself were speaking through you. Are you called to help others? Do it with all the strength and energy that God supplies. Then God will be given glory.

1 Peter 4:10–11 NLT

———

As God's grace brings more and more people to Christ, there will be great thanksgiving, and God will receive more and more glory.

2 Corinthians 4:15 NLT

———

Will you live for your own goals, comfort, and pleasure, or will you live the rest of your life for God's glory, knowing that he has promised eternal rewards?

All have sinned and fall short of the glory of God.
ROMANS 3:23 NIV

———

Anyone who holds on to life just as it is destroys that life. But if you let it go, reckless in your love, you'll have it forever, real and eternal.

JOHN 12:25 THE MESSAGE

———

Everything that goes into a life of pleasing God has been miraculously given to us by getting to know, personally and intimately, the One who invited us to God.

2 PETER 1:3 THE MESSAGE

———

To all who received Christ, to those who believed in his name, he gave the right to become children of God.

JOHN 1:12 NIV

———

Jesus said, "Whoever accepts and trusts the Son gets in on everything, life complete and forever!"

JOHN 3:36 THE MESSAGE

———

REFLECTIONS

_____

_____

_____

_____

_____

_____

_____

_____

_____

_____

_____

_____

_____

_____

_____

_____

_____

_____

_____

_____

Purpose 1:

YOU WERE PLANNED FOR GOD'S PLEASURE

❦

God has planted [his people] like strong and
graceful oaks for his own glory.
ISAIAH 61:3 LB

Planned for God's Pleasure

You, God, created everything, and it is for your
pleasure that they exist and were created.

REVELATION 4:11 NLT

The Lord takes pleasure in his people.

PSALM 149:4 TEV

The moment you were born into the world, God was there as an unseen witness, *smiling* at your birth.

Because of his love God had already decided that through Jesus Christ he would make us his children—this was his pleasure and purpose.

EPHESIANS 1:5 TEV

———

The LORD is pleased only with those who worship him and trust his love.

PSALM 147:11 CEV

———

Praise be to the LORD your God, who has delighted in you.

1 KINGS 10:9 NIV

———

Bringing pleasure to God is called "worship."

I will thank the LORD at all times.
   My mouth will always praise him.
         PSALM 34:1 GWT

The Father seeks worshipers.
         JOHN 4:23

Go to the Lord for help;
   and worship him continually.
         PSALM 105:4 TEV

Praise God from sunrise to sunset.
         PSALM 113:3 LB

God wants passion and commitment in our worship.

"These people come near to me with their mouth
   and honor me with their lips,
   but their hearts are far from me.
Their worship of me
   is made up only of rules taught by men,"
         says the Lord.
         ISAIAH 29:13 NIV

Every activity can be transformed into an act of worship when you do it for the praise, glory, and pleasure of God.

So whether you eat or drink or whatever you do, do it all for the glory of God.

1 CORINTHIANS 10:31 NIV

Whatever you do, work at it with all your heart, as working for the Lord, not for men.

COLOSSIANS 3:23 NIV

Take your everyday, ordinary life—your sleeping, eating, going-to-work, and walking-around life— and place it before God as an offering.

ROMANS 12:1 THE MESSAGE

REFLECTIONS

_____

_____

_____

_____

_____

_____

_____

_____

_____

_____

_____

_____

_____

_____

_____

_____

_____

_____

_____

What Makes God Smile

May the LORD smile on you.
NUMBERS 6:25 NLT

Smile on me, your servant;
teach me the right way to live.
PSALM 119:135 THE MESSAGE

Since pleasing God is the first purpose of your life, your most important task is to discover how to do that.

Figure out what will please Christ, and then do it.

EPHESIANS 5:10 THE MESSAGE

"I don't want your sacrifices—I want your love; I don't want your offerings—I want you to know me," says the LORD.

HOSEA 6:6 LB

Jesus said, "Love the Lord your God with all your heart and with all your soul and with all your mind. This is the first and greatest commandment."

MATTHEW 22:37–38 NIV

The Bible gives us a clear example of a life that gives pleasure to God. The man's name was Noah.

Noah consistently followed God's will and enjoyed a close relationship with him.
GENESIS 6:9 NLT

———

Noah did everything exactly as God had commanded him.
GENESIS 6:22 NLT

———

Noah built an altar to the LORD and, taking some of all the clean animals and clean birds, he and sacrificed burnt offerings on it.
GENESIS 8:20 NIV

———

By faith, Noah built a ship in the middle of dry land. He was warned about something he couldn't see, and acted on what he was told. . . . As a result, Noah became intimate with God.
HEBREWS 11:7 THE MESSAGE

———

Noah was a pleasure to the Lord.
GENESIS 6:8 LB

———

After the Flood, God gave Noah these simple instructions:

Be fruitful and increase in number and fill the earth. . . . Everything that lives and moves will be food for you. Just as I gave you the green plants, I now give you everything.
GENESIS 9:1, 3 NIV

God smiles when we love him supremely, trust him completely, obey him whole-heartedly, and praise and thank him continually.

God takes pleasure in those who honor him;
in those who trust in his constant love.
PSALM 147:11 TEV

Without faith it is impossible to please God because anyone who comes to him must believe that he exists and that he rewards those who earnestly seek him.
HEBREWS 11:6 NIV

Obey God gladly.
PSALM 100:2 LB

Just tell me what to do and I will do it, Lord.
As long as I live I'll wholeheartedly obey.
PSALM 119:33 LB

We please God by what we do and not only by what we believe.

JAMES 2:24 CEV

Jesus said, "If you love me, you will obey my commandments."

JOHN 14:15 TEV

By Christ therefore let us offer the sacrifice of praise to God continually, that is, the fruit of our lips giving thanks to his name.

HEBREWS 13:15 KJV

I will offer to thee the sacrifice of thanksgiving, and will call upon the name of the LORD.

PSALM 116:17 KJV

I will praise God's name in song
    and glorify him with thanksgiving.
This will please the LORD.

PSALM 69:30–31 NIV

The righteous are glad and rejoice in
        God's presence;
    they are happy and shout for joy.

PSALM 68:3 TEV

God smiles when we use our abilities. Every human activity, except sin, can be done for God's pleasure if you do it with an attitude of praise.

> The steps of the godly are directed by the LORD.
>> He delights in every detail of their lives.
>>> PSALM 37:23 NLT

———

> God has shaped each person in turn;
>> now he watches everything we do.
>>> PSALM 33:15 THE MESSAGE

———

God also gains pleasure in watching you enjoy his creation.

> God . . . generously gives us everything for our enjoyment.
>> 1 TIMOTHY 6:17 TEV

———

He knows you are incapable of being perfect or sinless.

God certainly knows what we are made of.
  He bears in mind that we are dust.
  PSALM 103:14 GWT

What God looks at is the attitude of your heart: Is pleasing him your deepest desire?

You have no right to argue with your Creator.
  You are merely a clay pot shaped by a potter.
The clay doesn't ask, "Why did you make me this
  way?"
  ISAIAH 45:9 CEV

More than anything else, however, we want to
please God, whether in our home here [on earth]
or there [in heaven].
  2 CORINTHIANS 5:9 TEV

The Lord looks down from heaven on all mankind
  to see if there are any who are wise, who
  want to please God.
  PSALM 14:2 LB

REFLECTIONS

_____

_____

_____

_____

_____

_____

_____

_____

_____

_____

_____

_____

_____

_____

_____

_____

_____

_____

_____

The Heart of Worship

Give yourselves to God, as those who have been
brought from death to life, and surrender your
whole being to him to be used for righteous
purposes.

ROMANS 6:13 TEV

DAILY INSPIRATION FOR THE PURPOSE-DRIVEN LIFE

The heart of worship is surrender. It is the natural response to God's amazing love and mercy.

This is how God showed his love among us: He sent his one and only Son into the world that we might live through him. This is love: not that we loved God, but that he loved us and sent his Son as an atoning sacrifice for our sins.

1 JOHN 4:9–10 NIV

We love because he first loved us.

1 JOHN 4: 19 NIV

God proves his love for us in that while we still were sinners Christ died for us.

ROMANS 5:8 NRSV

My friends, because of God's great mercy to us I appeal to you: Offer yourselves as a living sacrifice to God, dedicated to his service and pleasing to him. This is the true worship that you should offer.

ROMANS 12:1 TEV

Surrender means admitting our limitations. The desire to have complete control is the oldest temptation:

[The serpent said to Eve], "You'll be like God!"
GENESIS 3:5

I am the Lord's servant, and I am willing to accept whatever he wants.
LUKE 1:38 NLT

Surrendering is best demonstrated in obedience and trust.

After a night of failed fishing, Peter modeled surrender when Jesus told him to try again:

"Master, we've worked hard all night and haven't caught anything. But because you say so, I will let down the nets."
LUKE 5:5 NIV

Surrender yourself to the LORD and wait patiently for him.
PSALM 37:7 GWT

The night before his crucifixion, Jesus surrendered himself to God's plan. He prayed:

"Father, everything is possible for you. Please take this cup of suffering away from me. Yet I want your will, not mine."

MARK 14:36 NLT

The blessings of surrender are peace, freedom, and God's power in your life.

Stop quarreling with God! If you agree with him, you will have peace at last, and things will go well for you.

JOB 22:21 NLT

Offer yourselves to the ways of God and the freedom never quits. All your lives you've let sin tell you what to do. But thank God you've started listening to a new master, one whose commands set you free to live openly in his freedom!

ROMANS 6:17 THE MESSAGE

I am ready for anything and equal to anything through him who infuses inner strength into me, that is, I am self-sufficient in Christ's sufficiency.

PHILIPPIANS 4:13 AMP.

We make it our goal to please God.

2 CORINTHIANS 5:9 NIV

Give yourselves completely to God.
JAMES 4:7 NCV

**Surrendering is never just a one-time event.
You must make surrender a daily habit.**

I die every day.
1 CORINTHIANS 15:31

Jesus said, "If people want to follow me, they
must give up the things they want. They must be
willing to give up their lives daily to follow me."
LUKE 9:23 NCV

You cannot serve both God and money.
MATTHEW 6:24

"Do not store up for yourselves treasures on
earth, where moth and rust destroy, and where
thieves break in and steal. But store up for
yourselves treasures in heaven, where moth and
rust do not destroy, and where thieves do not
break in and steal. For where your treasure is,
there your heart will be also."
MATTHEW 6:19–21 NIV

DAILY INSPIRATION FOR THE PURPOSE-DRIVEN LIFE

REFLECTIONS

_____

_____

_____

_____

_____

_____

_____

_____

_____

_____

_____

_____

_____

_____

_____

_____

_____

_____

_____

_____

Becoming Best Friends with God

Since we were restored to friendship with God by
the death of his Son while we were still his
enemies, we will certainly be delivered from
eternal punishment by his life.

ROMANS 5:10 NLT

Friendship with God is possible only because of the grace of God and the sacrifice of Jesus.

Now we can rejoice in our wonderful new relationship with God—all because of what our Lord Jesus Christ has done for us in making us friends of God.

ROMANS 5:11 NLT

———

Anyone who is joined to Christ is a new being; the old is gone, the new has come. All this is done by God, who through Christ changed us from enemies into his friends.

2 CORINTHIANS 5:17–18 TEV

———

Jesus said, "I no longer call you servants, because a servant does not know his master's business. Instead, I have called you friends, for everything that I learned from my Father I have made known to you."

JOHN 15:15 NIV

———

God deeply desires that we know him intimately. In fact, he planned the universe and orchestrated history, including the details of our lives, so that we could become his friends.

He is a God who is passionate about his relationship with you.

EXODUS 34:14 NLT

God rules everything and is everywhere and is in everything.

EPHESIANS 4:6 NCV

God made the entire human race and made the earth hospitable, with plenty of time and space for living so we could seek after God, and not just grope around in the dark but actually find him.

ACTS 17:26–27 THE MESSAGE

"If any want to boast,
    they should boast that they know and
        understand me,
because my love is constant,
    and I do what is just and right.
These are the things that please me.
I, the Lord, have spoken."

JEREMIAH 9:24 TEV

God revealed himself to Samuel through his
word.

1 SAMUEL 3:21

**You can become a best friend of God through
constant conversation with him and through
continual meditation on his Word.**

Pray all the time.

1 THESSALONIANS 5:17 THE MESSAGE

I have treasured the words of God's mouth
   more than my daily bread.

JOB 23:12 NIV

Oh, how I love your law, LORD!
   I meditate on it all day long.

PSALM 119:97 NIV

Friendship with God is reserved for those who
reverence him. With them alone he shares the
secrets of his promises.

PSALM 25:14 LB

REFLECTIONS

_____

_____

_____

_____

_____

_____

_____

_____

_____

_____

_____

_____

_____

_____

_____

_____

_____

_____

_____

Developing Your Friendship
with God

God offers his friendship to the godly.
PROVERBS 3:32 NLT

Jesus ... friend of sinners.
MATTHEW 11:19 NIV

If you want a deeper, more intimate connection with God you must learn to honestly share your feelings with him.

Draw close to God, and God will draw close to you.

JAMES 4:8 NLT

———

[God told Job's friends,] "You haven't been honest either with me or about me—not the way my friend Job has. . . . My friend Job will now pray for you and I will accept his prayer."

JOB 42:7 THE MESSAGE

———

Moses was honest with God about his frustration over leading the Israelites:

"Look, you tell me to lead this people but you don't let me know whom you're going to send with me. . . . If I'm so special to you, let me in on your plans. . . . Don't forget, this is YOUR people, your responsibility. . . . If your presence doesn't take the lead here, call this trip off right now! How else will I know that you're with me in this, with me and your people? Are you traveling with us or not?". . . God said to Moses, "All right. Just as you say; this also I will do, for I know you well and you are special to me."

EXODUS 33:12–17 THE MESSAGE

———

I pour out my complaints before God and tell him
   all my troubles.
   For I am overwhelmed.
PSALM 142:2–3 NLT

**You must trust God when he asks you to do
something.**

Jesus said, "You are my friends if you do what I
command."
JOHN 15:14 NIV

Jesus said, "I have loved you even as the Father
has loved me. Remain in my love. When you obey
me, you remain in my love, just as I obey my
Father and remain in his love. I have told you this
so that you will be filled with my joy. Yes, your joy
will overflow!"
JOHN 15:9–11 NLT

What pleases the Lord more:
   burnt offerings and sacrifices or obedience?
It is better to obey God than to offer a sacrifice.

1 SAMUEL 15:22 NCV

Jesus is our example as a person who was obedient and pleased God:

Jesus went back to Nazareth with [his parents], and lived obediently with them.

LUKE 2:51 THE MESSAGE

[God spoke from heaven,]"This is my beloved Son, and I am fully pleased with him."

MATTHEW 3:17 NLT

To be a friend of God, you also need to learn to care about what he cares about.

Paul is the best example of this. God's agenda was his agenda, and God's passion was his:

The thing that has me so upset is that I care about you so much—this is the passion of God burning inside me!

2 CORINTHIANS 11:2 THE MESSAGE

David felt the same way:

Passion for your house, Lord, burns within me, so those who insult you are also insulting me.

PSALM 69:9 NLT

Your friendship with God will also develop when you learn to desire his friendship more than anything else.

The thing I seek most of all is the privilege
of meditating in God's Temple, living in his
presence every day of my life, delighting in
his incomparable perfections and glory.
PSALM 27:4 LB

Your love, LORD, means more than life to me.
PSALM 63:3 CEV

I will not let you go unless you bless me, LORD.
GENESIS 32:26 NIV

My determined purpose is that I may know Christ—that I may progressively become more deeply and intimately acquainted with Him, perceiving and recognizing and understanding the wonders of His Person more strongly and more clearly.

PHILIPPIANS 3:10 AMP.

"When you get serious about finding me and want it more than anything else, I'll make sure you won't be disappointed." GOD's Decree.

JEREMIAH 29:13 THE MESSAGE

There is nothing—absolutely nothing—more important than developing a friendship with God.

Some of these people have missed the most important thing in life—they don't know God.

1 TIMOTHY 6:21 LB

—— ✳ ——
REFLECTIONS

_____

_____

_____

_____

_____

_____

_____

_____

_____

_____

_____

_____

_____

_____

_____

_____

_____

_____

_____

_____

Worship That Pleases God

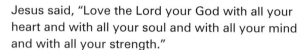

Jesus said, "Love the Lord your God with all your heart and with all your soul and with all your mind and with all your strength."

MARK 12:30 NIV

Let us be grateful and worship God in a way that will please him.

HEBREWS 12:28 TEV

The kind of worship that pleases God has four characteristics:

1. It is accurate.

Jesus said, "True worshipers will worship the Father in spirit and truth, for they are the kind of worshipers the Father seeks."

JOHN 4:23 NIV

———

2. It is authentic.

Man looks at the outward appearance, but the Lord looks at the heart.

1 SAMUEL 16:7 NIV

———

That's the kind of people the Father is out looking for: those who are simply and honestly themselves before him in their worship.

JOHN 4:23 THE MESSAGE

———

3. It is thoughtful.

Everything should be done in a fitting and orderly way.

1 CORINTHIANS 14:40 NIV

———

Suppose some strangers are in your worship service, when you are praising God with your spirit. If they don't understand you, how will they know to say, "Amen"? You may be worshiping God in a wonderful way, but no one else will be helped.

1 CORINTHIANS 14:16–17 CEV

———

4. It is practical.

Offer your bodies as living sacrifices, holy and pleasing to God—this is your spiritual act of worship.

ROMANS 12:1 NIV

———

I will not offer to the LORD my God sacrifices that have cost me nothing.

2 SAMUEL 24:24 TEV

———

REFLECTIONS

_____

_____

_____

_____

_____

_____

_____

_____

_____

_____

_____

_____

_____

_____

_____

_____

_____

_____

_____

_____

When God Seems Distant

The Lord has hidden himself from his people
but I trust him and place my hope in him.

ISAIAH 8:17 TEV

God is real, no matter how you feel. To mature your friendship, God will test it with periods of *seeming* separation—times when it feels as if he has abandoned or forgotten you.

Lord, why are you standing aloof and far away? Why do you hide when I need you the most?
PSALM 10:1 LB

———

Why have you forsaken me?
    Why do you remain so distant?
Why do you ignore my cries for help, LORD?
PSALM 22:1 NLT

———

Why have you abandoned me, God?
PSALM 43:2 TEV

———

But God doesn't leave you. He has promised repeatedly,

I will never leave you nor forsake you.
JOSHUA 1:5 NIV

———

God admits that sometimes he hides his face from us. This is a normal part of the testing and maturing of your friendship with God.

I go east, but he is not there.
  I go west, but I cannot find him.
I do not see him in the north, for he is hidden.
  I turn to the south, but I cannot find him.
But he knows where I am going.
  And when he has tested me like gold in a fire,
he will pronounce me innocent.

JOB 23:8–10 NLT

How do you praise God when you don't understand what's happening in your life and God is silent? You do what Job did:

Then he fell to the ground in worship and said:
"Naked I came from my mother's womb,
  and naked I will depart.
The LORD gave and the LORD has taken away;
  may the name of the LORD be praised."

JOB 1:20–21 NIV

Tell God exactly how you feel.

I can't be quiet!
   I am angry and bitter.
   I have to speak!
                    JOB 7:11 TEV

———

Oh, for the days when I was in my prime,
   when God's intimate friendship blessed my
      house.
                    JOB 29:4 NIV

———

I believed, so I said, "I am completely ruined!"
                    PSALM 116:10 NCV

———

This sounds like a contradiction: I trust God,
but I'm wiped out! David's frankness [in
Psalm 116:10] actually reveals a deep faith:
First, he believed in God. Second, he believed
God would listen to his prayer. Third, he
believed God would let him say what he felt
and still love him.

Regardless of circumstances and how you feel, hang on to God's unchanging character.

He is good and loving.

You gave me life and showed me kindness,
    and in your providence watched over my spirit.
JOB 10:12 NIV

———

He is all-powerful.

I know that you can do all things;
    no plan of yours can be thwarted.
JOB 42:2 NIV

———

He notices every detail of my life.

Does he not see my ways
    and count my every step?
JOB 31:4 NIV

———

He is in control.

Who appointed him over the earth?
    Who put him in charge of the whole world?
If it were his intention
    and he withdrew his spirit and breath,
all mankind would perish together
    and man would return to the dust.
JOB 34:13–15 NIV

———

He will save me.

I know that my Redeemer lives,
and that in the end he will stand upon the earth.
JOB 19:25 NIV

———

Circumstances cannot change the character of God. Trust God to keep his promises and remember what God has already done for you.

God may kill me, but still I will trust him.
JOB 13:15 CEV

———

I have not departed from the commands of
God's lips;
I have treasured the words of his mouth more
than my daily bread.
JOB 23:12 NIV

———

Christ was without sin, but for our sake God made him share our sin in order than in union with him we might share the righteousness of God.
2 CORINTHIANS 5:21 TEV

———

God has said,
"I will never leave you;
I will never abandon you."
HEBREWS 13:5 TEV

———

REFLECTIONS

_____

_____

_____

_____

_____

_____

_____

_____

_____

_____

_____

_____

_____

_____

_____

_____

_____

_____

_____

Purpose 2:

YOU WERE FORMED FOR GOD'S FAMILY

❧

Jesus said, "I am the vine, and you are the branches."

JOHN 15:5 CEV

Christ makes us one body ... connected to each other.

ROMANS 12:5 GWT

God is the One who made all things, and all things are for his glory. He wanted to have many children to share his glory.

HEBREWS 2:10 NCV

See how very much our heavenly Father loves us, for he allows us to be called his children, and we really are!

1 JOHN 3:1 NLT

Formed for God's Family

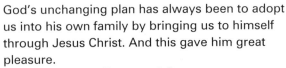

God's unchanging plan has always been to adopt
us into his own family by bringing us to himself
through Jesus Christ. And this gave him great
pleasure.

EPHESIANS 1:5 NLT

It was a happy day for him when he gave us our
new lives, through the truth of his Word, and we
became, as it were, the first children in his new
family.

JAMES 1:18 LB

God has given us the privilege of being born again,
so that we are now members of God's own family.

1 PETER 1:3 LB

When I think of the wisdom and scope of God's
plan I fall down on my knees and pray to the Father
of all the great family of God—some of them
already in heaven and some down here on earth.

EPHESIANS 3:14–15 LB

You are all children of God through faith in Christ
Jesus.

GALATIANS 3:26 NLT

The moment you were spiritually born into God's family, you were given some astounding birthday gifts: the family name, the family likeness, family privileges, family intimate access, and the family inheritance!

Since you are God's child, everything he has belongs to you.

GALATIANS 4:7 NLT

My God will meet all your needs according to his glorious riches in Christ Jesus.

PHILIPPIANS 4:19 NIV

I want you to realize what a rich and glorious inheritance God has given his people.

EPHESIANS 1:18 NLT

In him we have redemption through his blood, the forgiveness of sins, in accordance with the riches of God's grace.

EPHESIANS 1:7 NIV

God's kindness leads you toward repentance.

ROMANS 2:4 NIV

Oh, the depth of the riches of the wisdom and
knowledge of God!
How unsearchable his judgments,
and his paths beyond tracing out!

ROMANS 11:33 NIV

I pray that out of his glorious riches he may
strengthen you with power through his Spirit in
your inner being.

EPHESIANS 3:16 NIV

Because of his great love for us, God, who is rich
in mercy, made us alive with Christ even when we
were dead in transgressions—it is by grace you
have been saved.

EPHESIANS 2:4–5

God has reserved a priceless inheritance for his
children. It is kept in heaven for you, pure and
undefiled, beyond the reach of change and decay.

1 PETER 1:4 NLT

Healthy families have family pride; members are not ashamed to be recognized as part of the family. Baptism publicly announces to the world, "I am not ashamed to be a part of God's family."

Jesus said, "Go and make disciples of all the nations, baptizing them in the name of the Father and the Son and the Holy Spirit."

MATTHEW 28:19 NLT

———

Some of us are Jews, some are Gentiles, some are slaves, and some are free. But we have all been baptized into Christ's body by one Spirit, and we have all received the same Spirit.

1 CORINTHIANS 12:13 NLT

———

Whenever you feel unimportant, unloved, or insecure, remember to whom you belong.

Jesus and the people he makes holy all belong to the same family. That is why he isn't ashamed to call them his brothers and sisters.

HEBREWS 2:11 CEV

———

Jesus pointed to his disciples and said, "These are my mother and brothers. Anyone who does the will of my Father in heaven is my brother and sister and mother!"

MATTHEW 12:49–50 NLT

What Matters Most

No matter what I say, what I believe, and what I do, I'm bankrupt without love.

1 CORINTHIANS 13:3 THE MESSAGE

Love means living the way God commanded us to live. As you have heard from the beginning, his command is this: Live a life of love.

2 JOHN 1:6 NCV

Life is all about love. Because God is love, the most important lesson he wants you to learn on earth is how to love.

The whole Law can be summed up in this one command: "Love others as you love yourself."
GALATIANS 5:14 LB

———

Show special love for God's people.
1 PETER 2:17 CEV

———

When we have the opportunity to help anyone, we should do it. But we should give special attention to those who are in the family of believers.
GALATIANS 6:10 NCV

———

Jesus said, "Your strong love for each other will prove to the world that you are my disciples."
JOHN 13:35 LB

———

Let love be your greatest aim.
1 CORINTHIANS 14:1 LB

———

Love will last forever. God will evaluate us on our love in eternity.

These three things continue forever: faith, hope, and love. And the greatest of these is love.

1 CORINTHIANS 13:13 NCV

The only thing that counts is faith expressing itself through love.

GALATIANS 5:6 NIV

Be full of love for others, following the example of Christ who loved you and gave Himself to God as a sacrifice to take away your sins.

EPHESIANS 5:2 LB

God so loved the world that he gave his one and only Son, that whoever believes in him shall not perish but have eternal life.

JOHN 3:16 NIV

Jesus said the way to love him is to love his family and care for their practical needs:

"Truly I tell you, just as you did it to one of the least of these who are members of my family, you did it to me."

MATTHEW 25:40 NRSV

My children, our love should not be just words and talk; it must be true love, which shows itself in action.

1 JOHN 3:18 TEV

Because love is what matters most, it takes top priority.

Whenever we have the opportunity, we should do good to everyone.

GALATIANS 6:10 NLT

Use every chance you have for doing good.

EPHESIANS 5:16 NCV

Whenever you possibly can, do good to those who need it. Never tell your neighbor to wait until tomorrow if you can help them now.

PROVERBS 3:27 TEV

Jesus said, "'You must love the Lord your God with all your heart.' . . . This is the first and greatest commandment. A second is equally important: 'Love your neighbor as yourself.' All the other commandments and all the demands of the prophets are based on these two commandments."

MATTHEW 22:37–40 NLT

REFLECTIONS

_____

_____

_____

_____

_____

_____

_____

_____

_____

_____

_____

_____

_____

_____

_____

_____

_____

_____

A Place to Belong

———— ✑ ————

You are members of God's very own family,
citizens of God's country, and you belong in God's
household with every other Christian.

EPHESIANS 2:19 LB

———

God's family is the church of the living God, the
pillar and foundation of the truth.

1 TIMOTHY 3:15 GWT

———

We are created for community, fashioned for fellowship, and formed for a family, and none of us can fulfill God's purposes by ourselves. You are called to belong, not just believe.

God said, "It is not good for man to be alone."
GENESIS 2:18

In Christ we who are many form one body, and each member belongs to all the others.

ROMANS 12:5 NIV

In Christ the whole building is joined together and rises to become a holy temple in the Lord. And in him you too are being built together to become a dwelling in which God lives by his Spirit.
EPHESIANS 2:21–22 NIV

From Christ the whole body, joined and held together by every supporting ligament, grows and builds itself up in love, as each part does its work.

EPHESIANS 4:16 NIV

The body is a unit, though it is made up of many parts; and though all its parts are many, they form one body. For we were all baptized by one Spirit into one body—whether Jews or Greeks, slave or free—and we were all given the one Spirit to drink. Now the body is not made up of one part but of many. If the foot should say, "Because I am not a hand, I do not belong to the body," it would not for that reason cease to be part of the body. And if the ear should say, "Because I am not an eye, I do not belong to the body," it would not for that reason cease to be part of the body. If the whole body were an eye, where would the sense of hearing be? If the whole body were an ear, where would the sense of smell be? But in fact God has arranged the parts in the body, every one of them, just as he wanted them to be.

1 CORINTHIANS 12:12–18 NIV

———

Each part gets its meaning from the body as a whole, not the other way around. The body we're talking about is Christ's body of chosen people. Each of us finds our meaning and function as a part of his body. But as a chopped-off finger of cut-off toe we wouldn't amount to much, would we?

ROMANS 12:4–5 THE MESSAGE

———

Membership in the family of God is neither inconsequential nor something to be casually ignored. The church is God's agenda for the world.

Jesus said, "I will build my church, and all the powers of hell will not conquer it."
MATTHEW 16:18 NLT

———

Christ loved the church and gave his life for it. He did this to make the church holy by cleansing it, washing it using water along with spoken words. Then he could present it to himself as a glorious church, without any kind of stain or wrinkle—holy and without faults.
EPHESIANS 5:25–27 GWT

———

Love your spiritual family.
1 PETER 2:17 THE MESSAGE

———

You need your church family because it identifies you as a genuine believer, moves you out of self-centered isolation, and helps you develop spiritual muscle.

Jesus said, "Your love for one another will prove to the world that you are my disciples."
JOHN 13:35 NLT

Jesus prayed, "My prayer is not for [my disciples] alone. I pray also for those who will believe in me through their message, that all of them may be one, Father, just as you are in me and I am in you. May they also be in us so that the world may believe that you have sent me."
JOHN 17:20–21 NIV

If one part of the body suffers, all the other parts suffer with it. Or if one part of our body is honored, all the other parts share its honor.
1 CORINTHIANS 12:26 NCV

Jesus laid down his life for us. And we ought to lay down our lives for our brothers.
1 JOHN 3:16 NIV

As each part does its own special work, it helps the other parts grow, so that the whole body is healthy and growing and full of love.
EPHESIANS 4:16 NLT

Not only do you need the body of Christ, the body of Christ needs you. You are a part of Christ's mission in the world.

A spiritual gift is given to each of us as a means of helping the entire church. To one person the Spirit gives the ability to give wise advice; to another he gives the gift of special knowledge. The Spirit gives special faith to another, and to someone else he gives the power to heal the sick. He gives one person the power to perform miracles, and to another the ability to prophesy. He gives someone else the ability to know whether it is really the Spirit of God or another spirit that is speaking. Still another person is given the ability to speak in unknown languages, and another is given the ability to interpret what is being said. It is the one and only Holy Spirit who distributes these gifts. He alone decides which gift each person should have.

1 CORINTHIANS 12:7–11 NLT

God creates each of us by Christ Jesus to join him in the work he does, the good work he has gotten ready for us to do, work we had better be doing.

EPHESIANS 2:10 THE MESSAGE

None of us are immune to temptation. God knows this, so he has assigned us as individuals the responsibility of keeping each other on track.

Encourage one another daily, as long as it is called Today, so that none of you may be hardened by sin's deceitfulness.

HEBREWS 3:13 NIV

———

If you know people who have wandered off from God's truth, don't write them off. Go after them. Get them back.

JAMES 5:19 THE MESSAGE

———

[The church leaders'] work is to watch over your souls, and they know they are accountable to God.

HEBREWS 13:17 NLT

———

The Christian life if more than just commitment to Christ; it includes a commitment to other Christians.

First they gave themselves to the Lord; and then, by God's will, they gave themselves to us as well.

2 CORINTHIANS 8:5 TEV

———

REFLECTIONS

_____

_____

_____

_____

_____

_____

_____

_____

_____

_____

_____

_____

_____

_____

_____

_____

_____

_____

_____

Experiencing Life Together

Each one of you is part of the body of Christ, and
you were chosen to live together in peace.

COLOSSIANS 3:15 CEV

How wonderful it is, how pleasant,
    for God's people to live together in harmony!

PSALM 133:1 TEV

God intends for us to experience life together. The Bible calls this shared experience *fellowship.*

Jesus said, "Where two or three have gathering together in My name, I am there in their midst."

MATTHEW 18:20 NASB

———

Two are better than one,
   because together they can work effectively.
If one of them falls down,
   the other can help him up. . . .
Two people can resist an attack
   that would defeat one person alone.
A rope made of three cords is hard to break.

ECCLESIASTES 4:9 TEV

———

In real fellowship people experience authenticity.

If we live in the light, as God is in the light, we can share fellowship with each other. And when we live in the light, the blood of the death of Jesus, God's Son, is making us clean of every sin. If we say we have no sin, we are fooling ourselves, and the truth is not in us.

1 JOHN 1:7–8 NCV

———

Make this your common practice: Confess your
sins to each other and pray for each other so that
you can live together whole and healed.

JAMES 5:16 THE MESSAGE

———

**In real fellowship people experience
mutuality—the art of giving and receiving.**

The way God designed our bodies is a model for
understanding our lives together as a church:
every part dependent on every other part.

1 CORINTHIANS 12:25 THE MESSAGE

———

I want us to help each other with the faith we
have. Your faith will help me, and my faith will
help you.

ROMANS 1:12 NCV

———

Love one another with mutual affection; outdo
one another in showing honor.

ROMANS 12:10 NRSV

———

Make every effort to do what leads to peace and
to mutual edification.

ROMANS 14:19 NIV

———

In real fellowship people experience sympathy.

As holy people whom God has chosen and loved, be sympathetic, kind, humble, gentle, and patient.

COLOSSIANS 3:12 GWT

———

Share each other's troubles and problems and in this way obey the law of Christ.

GALATIANS 6:2 NLT

———

A despairing man should have the devotion of his friends,
even though he forsakes the fear of the Almighty.

JOB 6:14 NIV

———

In real fellowship people experience mercy.

When people sin, you should forget and comfort
them, so they won't give up in despair.
2 CORINTHIANS 2:7 CEV

Never hold grudges.
COLOSSIANS 3:13 LB

You must make allowance for each other's
faults and forgive the person who offends you.
Remember, the Lord forgave you, so you must
forgive others.
COLOSSIANS 3:13 NLT

REFLECTIONS

Cultivating Community

You can develop a healthy, robust community that lives right with God and enjoy its results only if you do the hard work of getting along with each other, treating each other with dignity and honor.

JAMES 3:18 THE MESSAGE

[The first Christians] committed themselves to the teaching of the apostles, the life together, the common meal, and the prayers.

ACTS 2:42 THE MESSAGE

Community requires commitment. Only the Holy Spirit can create real fellowship between believers, but he cultivates it with the choices and commitments we make.

You are joined together with peace through the Spirit, so make every effort to continue together in this way.

EPHESIANS 4:3 NCV

———

The New Testament is filled with instruction on how to share life together.

I am writing these things to you ... [so] you will know how to live in the family of God. That family is the church.

1 TIMOTHY 3:14–15 NCV

———

Cultivating community takes honesty.

Speaking the truth in love, we will in all things grow up into him who is the Head, that is, Christ.

EPHESIANS 4:15 NIV

———

Brothers and sisters, if someone in your group does something wrong, you who are spiritual should go to that person and gently make him right again.

GALATIANS 6:1–2 NCV

———

An honest answer is a true sign of friendship.
PROVERBS 24:26 TEV

———

No more lies, no more pretense. Tell your
neighbor the truth. In Christ's body we're all
connected to each other, after all. When you lie to
others, you end up lying to yourself.

EPHESIANS 4:25 THE MESSAGE

———

In the end, people appreciate frankness more than
flattery.
PROVERBS 28:23 NLT

———

You must not simply look the other way and hope
[immorality] goes away on its own. Bring it out in
the open and deal with it. . . . Better devastation
and embarrassment than damnation. . . . You pass
if off as a small thing, but it's anything but that. . . .
You shouldn't act as if everything is just fine when
one of your Christian companions is promiscuous
or crooked, is flip with God or rude to friends,
gets drunk or becomes greedy and predatory.
You can't just go along with this, treating it as
acceptable behavior. I'm not responsible for what
the outsiders do, but don't we have some
responsibility for those within our community of
believers?

1 CORINTHIANS 5:3–12 THE MESSAGE

———

Never use harsh words when you correct an older man, but talk to him as if he were your father. Talk to younger men as if they were your brothers, older women as if they were your mothers, and younger women as if they were your sisters.

1 TIMOTHY 5:1–2 GWT

———

Cultivating community takes humility.

Clothe yourselves with humility toward one another because God opposes the proud, but gives grace to the humble.

1 PETER 5:5 NIV

———

Live in harmony with each other. Don't try to act important, but enjoy the company of ordinary people. And don't think you know it all!

ROMANS 12:16 NLT

———

Give more honor to others than to yourselves. Do not be interested only in your own life, but be interested in the lives of others.

PHILIPPIANS 2:3–4 NCV

———

Cultivating community takes courtesy.

We must bear the "burden" of being considerate of the doubts and fears of others.

ROMANS 15:2 LB

God's people should be bighearted and courteous.

TITUS 3:2 THE MESSAGE

Be devoted to each other like a loving family. Excel in showing respect for each other.

ROMANS 12:10 GWT

Cultivating community takes confidentiality.

Gossip is spread by wicked people;
   they stir up trouble and break up friendships.

PROVERBS 16:28 TEV

Warn a divisive person once, and then warn him a second time. After that, have nothing to do with him.

TITUS 3:10 NIV

Cultivating community takes frequency.

Let us not give up the habit of meeting together,
as some are doing. Instead, let us encourage one
another.

HEBREWS 10:25 TEV

———

[The first Christians] worshiped together regularly
at the Temple each day, met in small groups in
homes for Communion, and shared their meals
with great joy and thankfulness.

ACTS 2:46 LB

———

We understand what love is when we realize that
Christ gave his life for us. That means we must
give our lives for other believers.

1 JOHN 3:16 GWT

———

REFLECTIONS

_____

_____

_____

_____

_____

_____

_____

_____

_____

_____

_____

_____

_____

_____

_____

_____

_____

_____

_____

Restoring Broken Fellowship

— ❧ —

God has restored our relationship with him
through Christ, and has given us this ministry
of restoring relationships.

2 CORINTHIANS 5:18 GWT

Relationships are always worth restoring. God has given us the ministry of restoring relationships. For this reason a significant amount of the New Testament is devoted to teaching us how to get along with one another.

If you've gotten anything at all out of following Christ, if his love has made any difference in your life, if being in a community of the Spirit means anything to you, if you have a heart, if you care— then do me a favor: Agree with each other, love each other, be deep-spirited friends.

PHILIPPIANS 2:1–2 THE MESSAGE

Shame on you! Surely there is at least one wise person in your fellowship who can settle a dispute between fellow Christians.

1 CORINTHIANS 6:5 TEV

I'll put it as urgently as I can: You must get along with each other.

1 CORINTHIANS 1:10 THE MESSAGE

Jesus said, "God blesses those who work for peace, for they will be called the children of God."

MATTHEW 5:9 NLT

You are only hurting yourself with your anger.

JOB 18:4 TEV

God has called us to settle our relationships with each other.

2 CORINTHIANS 5:18 THE MESSAGE

Here are seven biblical steps to restoring fellowship:

1. Talk to God before talking to the person.

What causes fights and quarrels among you? Don't they come from your desires that battle within in? You want something but don't get it. You kill and covet, but you cannot have what you want. You quarrel and fight. You do not have, because you do not ask God.

JAMES 4:1–2 NIV

---

2. Always take the initiative.

Jesus said, "If you enter your place of worship and, about to make an offering, you suddenly remember a grudge a friend has against you, abandon your offering, leave immediately, go to this friend and make things right. Then and only then, come back and work things out with God."

MATTHEW 5:23–24 THE MESSAGE

---

3. Sympathize with their feelings.

Look out for another's interests, not just for your own.

PHILIPPIANS 2:4 TEV

A man's wisdom gives him patience;
    it is to his glory to overlook an offense.

PROVERBS 19:11 NIV

Let's please the other fellow, not ourselves, and do what is for his good.

ROMANS 15:2 LB

Do not use harmful words, but only helpful words, the kind that build up and provide what is needed, so that what you say will do good to those who hear you.

EPHESIANS 4:29 TEV

---

4. Confess your part of the conflict.

Jesus said, "First get rid of the log from your own eye; then perhaps you will see well enough to deal with the speck in your friend's eye."

MATTHEW 7:5 NLT

If we claim that we're free of sin, we're only fooling ourselves.

1 JOHN 1:8 THE MESSAGE

---

5. Attack the problem, not the person.

When my thoughts were bitter
    and my feelings were hurt,
I was as stupid as an animal.

PSALM 73:21–22 TEV

A gentle response defuses anger,
    but a sharp tongue kindles a temper-fire.

PROVERBS 15:1 THE MESSAGE

A wise, mature person is known for his
    understanding.
The more pleasant his words, the more
    persuasive he is.

PROVERBS 16:21 TEV

---

6. *Cooperate as much as possible.*

Do everything possible on your part to live in peace with everybody.

ROMANS 12:18 TEV

———

You're blessed when you can show people how to cooperate instead of compete or fight. That's when you discover who you really are, and your place in God's family.

MATTHEW 5:9 THE MESSAGE

———

7. *Emphasize reconciliation, not resolution.*

Work hard at living at peace with others.

1 PETER 3:11 NLT

———

Jesus said, "Blessed are the peacemakers, for they will be called sons of God."

MATTHEW 5:9 NIV

———

Christ did not indulge his own feelings . . . as Scripture says: The insults of those who insult you fall on me.

ROMANS 15:3 NJB

———

REFLECTIONS

DAILY INSPIRATION FOR THE PURPOSE-DRIVEN LIFE

Protecting Your Church

You are joined together with peace through the Spirit, so make every effort to continue together in this way.

EPHESIANS 4:3 NCV

Most of all, let love guide your life, for then the whole church will stay together in perfect harmony.

COLOSSIANS 3:14 LB

God deeply desires that we experience oneness and harmony with each other. Unity is the soul of fellowship.

———

Make every effort to keep the unity of the Spirit through the bond of peace.

EPHESIANS 4:3 NIV

———

Don't think only of your own good. Think of other Christians and what is best for them.

1 CORINTHIANS 10:24 NLT

———

How are we to do this? The Bible gives us practical advice.

1. Focus on what we have in common, not our differences.

Let us concentrate on the things which make for harmony, and on the growth of one another's character.

ROMANS 14:19 PH.

———

Let there be real harmony so there won't be divisions in the church. I plead with you to be of one mind united in though and purpose.

1 CORINTHIANS 1:10 NLT

———

2. Be realistic in your expectations.

Be patient with each other, making allowance for each other's faults because of your love.

EPHESIANS 4:2 NLT

———

3. Choose to encourage rather than criticize.

What right do you have to criticize someone else's servants? Only their Lord can decide if they are doing right.

ROMANS 14:4 CEV

———

Why, then, criticize your brother's actions, why try to make him look small? We shall all be judged one day, not by each other's standards or even our own, but by the standard of Christ.

ROMANS 14:10 PH.

———

Let's agree to use all our energy in getting along with each other. Help others with encouraging words; don't drag them down by finding fault.

ROMANS 14:19 THE MESSAGE

———

A critical spirit is a costly vice. The Bible calls Satan "the accuser of our brothers" (Revelation 12:10). No matter how much to disagree with other Christians, they are not the real enemy.

4. Refuse to listen to gossip.

Troublemakers listen to troublemakers.
PROVERBS 17:4 CEV

———

In the last days there will be people who don't take [God's commands] seriously anymore.... These are the ones who split churches, thinking only of themselves.
JUDE 1:18–19 THE MESSAGE

———

A gossip reveals secrets;
    therefore do not associate with a babbler.

PROVERBS 20:19 NRSV

———

Paul warned about "cannibal Christians" who "devour one another" (Galatians 5:15 Amp) and destroy the fellowship. The Bible says these kind of troublemakers should be avoided.

Fire goes out for lack of fuel,
    and tensions disappear when gossip stops.

PROVERBS 26:20 LB

———

5. Practice God's method for conflict resolution.

If a fellow believer hurts you, go and tell him—
work it out between the two of you. If he listens,
you've made a friend. If he won't listen, take one
or two others along so that the presence of
witnesses will keep things honest, and try again. If
he still won't listen, tell the church.

MATTHEW 18:15–17 THE MESSAGE

6. Support your pastor and leaders.

Be responsive to your pastoral leaders. Listen to
their counsel. They are alert to the condition of
your lives and work under the strict supervision of
God. Contribute to the joy of their leadership, not
its drudgery. Why would you want to make things
harder for them?

HEBREWS 13:17 THE MESSAGE

[Pastors] keep watch over you as men who must
give an account.

HEBREWS 13:17 NIV

Honor those leaders who work so hard for you,
who have been given the responsibility of urging
and guiding you along in your obedience.
Overwhelm them with appreciation and love!

1 THESSALONIANS 5:12–13 THE MESSAGE

REFLECTIONS

_____

_____

_____

_____

_____

_____

_____

_____

_____

_____

_____

_____

_____

_____

_____

_____

_____

_____

Purpose 3:

YOU WERE CREATED TO BECOME LIKE CHRIST

Let your roots grow down into Christ and draw up
nourishment from him. See that you go on
growing in the Lord, and become strong and
vigorous in the truth.

COLOSSIANS 2:7 LB

Created to Become Like Christ

God knew what he was doing from the very beginning. He decided from the outset to shape the lives of those who love him along the same lines as the life of his Son. The Son stands first in the line of humanity he restored. We see the original and intended shape of our lives there in him.

ROMANS 8:29 THE MESSAGE

We look at this Son and see God's original purpose in everything created.

COLOSSIANS 1:15 THE MESSAGE

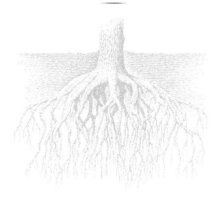

From the very beginning, God's plan has been to make you like his Son, Jesus.

Then God said, " Let us make human beings in our image and likeness."

GENESIS 1:26 NCV

What does the full "image and likeness" of God look like? It looks like Jesus Christ! The Bible says:
[Jesus is] the exact likeness of God.

2 CORINTHIANS 4:4 NLT

[Jesus is] the visible image of the invisible God.

COLOSSIANS 1:15 NLT

[Jesus is] the exact representation of God's being.

HEBREWS 1:3 NIV

You were also taught to become a new person created to be like God, truly righteous and holy.

EPHESIANS 4:24 GWT

God doesn't want you to become a god; he wants you to become *godly*—taking on his values, attitudes, and character.

Take on an entirely new way of life—a God-fashioned life, a life renewed from the inside and working itself into your conduct as God accurately reproduces his character in you.

EPHESIANS 4:22 THE MESSAGE

It is the Holy Spirit's job to produce Christlike character in you.

As the Spirit of the Lord works within us, we become more and more like him and reflect his glory even more.

2 CORINTHIANS 3:18 NLT

God is working in you, giving you the desire to obey him and the power to do what pleases him.

PHILIPPIANS 2:13 NLT

The Holy Spirit often nudges us with "a gentle whisper" (1 Kings 19:12 NIV).

Christlikeness is not produced by imitation, but by inhabitation.

For this is the secret: Christ lives in you.

COLOSSIANS 1:27 NLT

While effort has nothing to do with your salvation, it has much to do with your spiritual growth. We must cooperate with the Holy Spirit's work in our lives. At least eight times in the New Testament we are told to "make every effort" in our growth toward becoming like Jesus.

Jesus said, "Make every effort to enter through the narrow door [to follow Christ], because many, I tell you, will try to enter and will not be able to."

LUKE 13:24 NIV

———

Make every effort to give yourself to God as the kind of person he will accept. Be a worker who is not ashamed and who uses the true teaching in the right way.

2 TIMOTHY 2:15 NCV

———

Make every effort to live in peace with all men and to be holy; without holiness no one will see the Lord.

HEBREWS 12:14 NIV

———

Make every effort to add to your faith goodness; and to goodness, knowledge; and to knowledge, self-control; and to self-control, perseverance; and to perseverance, godliness; and to godliness, brotherly kindness; and to brotherly kindness, love.

2 PETER 1:5–7 NIV

In keeping with God's promise we are looking forward to a new heaven and a new earth, the home of righteousness. So then, dear friends, since you are looking forward to this, make every effort to be found spotless, blameless and at peace with him.

2 PETER 3:13–14 NIV

We have three responsibilities in becoming like Christ.

First, we must choose to let go of old ways of acting.

Everything—and I do mean everything—connected with [your] old way of life has to go. It's rotten through and through. Get rid of it!

EPHESIANS 4:22 THE MESSAGE

Second, we must change the way we think.

Let the Spirit change your way of thinking.

EPHESIANS 4:23 CEV

Third, we must "put on" the character of Christ by developing new godly habits.

Put on the new self, created to be like God in true righteousness and holiness.

EPHESIANS 4:24 NIV

Spiritual maturity is neither instant nor automatic; it is a gradual, progressive development that will take the rest of your life. Becoming like Christ is a long, slow process of growth.

[This process of becoming Christlike] will continue until we are united by our faith and by our understanding of the Son of God. Then we will be mature, just as Christ is, and we will be completely like him.

EPHESIANS 4:13 CEV

We can't even imagine what we will be like when Christ returns. But we do know that when he comes we will be like him, for we will see him as he really is.

1 JOHN 3:2 NLT

Don't become so well-adjusted to your culture that you fit into it without even thinking. Instead, fix your attention on God. You'll be changed from the inside out. Readily recognize what he wants from you, and quickly respond to it. Unlike the culture around you, always dragging you down to its level of immaturity, God brings the best out of you, develops well-formed maturity in you.

ROMANS 12:2 THE MESSAGE

REFLECTIONS

_____

_____

_____

_____

_____

_____

_____

_____

_____

_____

_____

_____

_____

_____

_____

_____

_____

_____

_____

_____

How We Grow

_____ ℳ _____

God wants us to grow up, to know the whole truth
and tell it in love—like Christ in everything.

EPHESIANS 4:15 THE MESSAGE

_____

We are not meant to remain as children.

EPHESIANS 4:14 PH.

_____

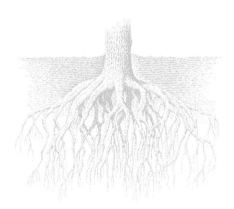

Discipleship—the process of becoming like Christ—always begins with a decision.

"Come, be my disciple," Jesus said to him. So Matthew got up and followed him.

MATTHEW 9:9 NLT

———

Once you decide to get serious about becoming like Christ, you must begin to act in new ways. You can be certain that the Holy Spirit will help you with these changes.

———

Continue to work out your salvation with fear and trembling, for it is God who works in you to will and to act according to his good purpose.

PHILIPPIANS 2:12–13 NIV

———

The "*work out*" is your responsibility, and the "*work in*" is God's role.

Your first step in spiritual growth is to start changing the way you think. The way you think determines the way you feel, and the way you feel influences the way you act.

Be careful how you think;
    your life is shaped by your thoughts.
                            PROVERBS 4:23 TEV

Let God transform you into a new person by changing the way you think. Then you will know what God wants you to do.

                            ROMANS 12:2 NLT

There must be a spiritual renewal of your thoughts and attitudes.
                            EPHESIANS 4:23 NLT

Think the same way that Christ Jesus thought.
                            PHILIPPIANS 2:5 CEV

Stop thinking like children. In regard to evil be infants, but in your thinking be adults.
                            1 CORINTHIANS 14:20 NIV

Since everything around us is going to melt away, what holy, godly lives you should be living!
                            2 PETER 3:11 NLT

Those who live following their sinful selves think
only about things that their sinful selves want. But
those who live following the Spirit are thinking
about the things the Spirit wants them to do.

ROMANS 8:5 NCV

———

When I was a child, I talked like a child, I thought
like a child, I reasoned like a child. When I became
a man, I put childish ways behind me.

1 CORINTHIANS 13:11 NIV

———

We should think of [our neighbors'] good and try
to help them by doing what pleases them. Even
Christ did not try to please himself.

ROMANS 15:2–3 CEV

———

God has given us his Spirit. That's why we don't
think the same way that the people of the world
think.

1 CORINTHIANS 2:12 CEV

———

Let God transform you inwardly by a complete
change of your mind. Then you will be able to
know the will of God—what is good and is
pleasing to him and is perfect.

ROMANS 12:2 TEV

———

REFLECTIONS

_____

_____

_____

_____

_____

_____

_____

_____

_____

_____

_____

_____

_____

_____

_____

_____

_____

_____

_____

Transformed by Truth

Jesus said, "People need more than bread for their life; they must feed on every word of God."

MATTHEW 4:4 NLT

Now I am turning you over to God, our marvelous God whose gracious Word can make you into what he wants you to be and give you everything you could possibly need in this community of holy friends.

ACTS 20:32 THE MESSAGE

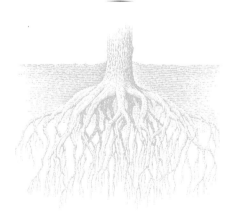

Spiritual growth is the process of replacing lies with truth. The Spirit of God uses the Word of God to make us like the Son of God. To become like Jesus, we must fill our lives with his Word.

Jesus prayed, "Sanctify [my followers] by the truth; your word is truth."

JOHN 17:17 NIV

———

Through the Word we are put together and shaped up for the tasks God has for us.

2 TIMOTHY 3:17 THE MESSAGE

———

Jesus said, "The words that I have spoken to you are spirit and are life."

JOHN 6:63 NASB

———

God's Word is unlike any other word. Without God's Word you would not even be alive.

The word of God is living and active. Sharper than any double-edged sword, it penetrates even to dividing soul and spirit, joints and marrow; it judges the thoughts and attitudes of the heart.

HEBREWS 4:12 NIV

───────

You have been born again, not of perishable seed, but of imperishable, through the living and enduring word of God.

1 PETER 1:23 NIV

───────

God decided to give us life through the word of truth so we might be the most important of all the things he made.

JAMES 1:18 NCV

───────

God's Word is the spiritual nourishment you _must_ have to fulfill your purpose.

I have treasured the words of God's mouth
more than my daily bread.

JOB 23:12 NIV

Crave pure spiritual milk, so that by it you may
grow up in your salvation.

1 PETER 2:2 NIV

Jesus said, "Man does not live on bread alone,
but on every word that comes from the mouth
of God."

MATTHEW 4:4 NIV

How sweet are your words to my taste, LORD,
sweeter than honey to my mouth!

PSALM 119:103 NIV

To be a healthy disciple of Jesus, feeding on God's Word must be your first priority.

Jesus said, "If you abide in My word, then you are truly disciples of Mine."
JOHN 8:31 NASB

———

In day-to-day living, abiding in God's Word includes three activities.

1. Accepting the Bible's authority.

Every word of God is flawless.
PROVERBS 30:5 NIV

———

Everything in the Scriptures is God's Word. All of it is useful for teaching and helping people and for correcting them and showing them how to live.
2 TIMOTHY 3:16 CEV

———

I believe everything that agrees with the Law and that is written in the Prophets.
. ACTS 24:14 NIV

———

2. Assimilating the Bible's truth.

Receive it:

Jesus said, "There is nothing hidden that will not be disclosed, and nothing concealed that will not be known or brought out into the open. Therefore consider carefully how you listen."

LUKE 8:17–18 NIV

—

In a humble (gentle, modest) spirit, receive and welcome the Word which implanted and rooted in your hearts contains the power to save your souls.

JAMES 1:21 AMP.

—

Read it:

Daily Bible reading will keep you in range of God's voice. This is why God instructed the kings of Israel to always keep a copy of his Word nearby:

He should keep it with him all the time and read from it every day of his life.

DEUTERONOMY 17:19 NCV

—

Research it:

Truly happy people are those who carefully study God's perfect law that makes people free, and they continue to study it. They do not forget what they heard, but they obey what God's teaching says. Those who do this will be made happy.

JAMES 1:25 NCV

Remember it:

Remember what Christ taught and let his words enrich your lives and make you wise.

COLOSSIANS 3:16 LB

I have hidden your word in my heart, LORD,
  that I might not sin against you.

PSALM 119:11 NIV

Your word is a lamp to my feet
  and a light for my path, O God.

PSALM 119:105 NIV

When your words came, I ate them;
  they were my joy and my heart's delight,
for I bear your name,
  O LORD God Almighty.

JEREMIAH 15:16 NIV

Reflect on it:

How I love your teachings, LORD!
　I think about them all day long.
　　　　　　　　PSALM 119:97 NCV

———

Do not let this Book of the Law depart from your mouth; meditate on it day and night, so that you may be careful to do everything written in it. Then you will be prosperous and successful.
　　　　　　　　JOSHUA 1:8 NIV

———

Blessed is the man
　who does not walk in the counsel of the wicked
or stand in the way of sinners
　or sit in the seat of mockers.
But his delight is in the law of the LORD,
　and on his law he meditates day and night.
He is like a tree planted by streams of water,
　which yields its fruit in season
and whose leaf does not wither.
　Whatever he does prospers.
　　　　　　　　PSALM 1:1–3 NIV

———

We, who with unveiled faces all reflect the Lord's glory, are being transformed into his likeness with ever-increasing glory, which comes from the Lord, who is the Spirit.
　　　　　　　　2 CORINTHIANS 3:18 NIV

———

3. Apply the Bible's principles.

Jesus said, "Everyone who hears these words of mine and puts them into practice is like a wise man who built his home on the rock."

MATTHEW 7:24 NIV

———

Be doers of the word, and not hearers only.

JAMES 1:22 KJV

———

When Jesus had finished washing [his disciples'] feet, he put on his clothes and returned to his place. "Do you understand what I have done for you?" he asked them. "You call me 'Teacher' and 'Lord,' and rightly so, for that is what I am. Now that I, your Lord and Teacher, have washed your feet, you also should wash one another's feet. I have set you an example that you should do as I have done for you. I tell you the truth, no servant is greater than his master, nor is a messenger greater than the one who sent him. Now that you know these things, you will be blessed if you do them."

JOHN 13:12–17 NIV

———

Jesus said, "If ye continue in my word, then are ye my disciples indeed; and ye shall know the truth and the truth shall make you free."

JOHN 8:31–32 KJV

———

REFLECTIONS

_____

_____

_____

_____

_____

_____

_____

_____

_____

_____

_____

_____

_____

_____

_____

_____

_____

_____

_____

_____

Transformed by Trouble

For our light and momentary troubles are achieving for us an eternal glory that far outweighs them all.

2 CORINTHIANS 4:17 NIV

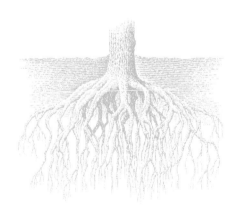

God has a purpose behind every problem.

Don't be bewildered or surprised when you go through the fiery trials ahead, for this is no strange, unusual thing that is going to happen to you.

1 PETER 4:12 LB

Jesus said, "In this world you will have trouble. But take heart! I have overcome the world."

JOHN 16:33 NIV

God uses problems to draw you closer to himself.

The Lord is close to the brokenhearted;
    he rescues those who are crushed in spirit.

PSALM 34:18 NLT

We learn things about God in suffering that we can't learn any other way.

God could have kept Joseph out of jail:

Joseph's master took him and put him in prison, the place where the king's prisoners were confined. But while Joseph was there in the prison, the LORD was with him; he showed him kindness and granted him favor in the eyes of the prison warden. So the warden put Joseph in charge of all those held in the prison, and he was made responsible for all that was done there. The warden paid no attention to anything under Joseph's care, because the LORD was with Joseph and gave him success in whatever he did.

GENESIS 39:20–23 NIV

God could have kept Jeremiah from being tossed into a slimy pit:

[The king's officials] took Jeremiah and put him into the cistern of Malkijah, the king's son, which was in the courtyard of the guard. They lowered Jeremiah by ropes into the cistern; it had no water in it, only mud, and Jeremiah sank down into the mud.

JEREMIAH 38:6 NIV

God could have kept Daniel out of the lion's den:

The king gave the order, and they brought
Daniel and threw him into the lions' den. The king
said to Daniel, "May your God, whom
you serve continually, rescue you!" A stone was
brought and placed over the mouth of the den,
and the king sealed it with his own signet ring
and with the rings of his nobles, so that Daniel's
situation might not be changed. Then the king
returned to his palace and spent the night without
eating and without any entertainment being
brought to him. And he could not sleep. At the
first light of dawn, the king got up and hurried
to the lions' den. When he came near the den, he
called to Daniel in an anguished voice, "Daniel,
servant of the living God, has your God, whom
you serve continually, been able to rescue you
from the lions?" Daniel answered, "O king, live
forever! My God sent his angel, and he shut the
mouths of the lions. They have not hurt me,
because I was found innocent in his sight. Nor
have I ever done any wrong before you, O king."
The king was overjoyed and gave orders to lift
Daniel out of the den. And when Daniel was lifted
from the den, no wound was found on
him, because he had trusted in his God.

DANIEL 6:16–23 NIV

God could have kept Paul from being shipwrecked three times:

Three times I was beaten with rods, once I was stoned, three times I was shipwrecked, I spent a night and a day in the open sea, I have been constantly on the move. I have been in danger from rivers, in danger from bandits, in danger from my own countrymen, in danger from Gentiles; in danger in the city, in danger in the country, in danger at sea; and in danger from false brothers. I have labored and toiled and have often gone without sleep; I have known hunger and thirst and have often gone without food; I have been cold and naked.

2 CORINTHIANS 11:25–27 NIV

God could have kept the three Hebrew young men from being thrown into the blazing furnace:

Shadrach, Meshach and Abednego replied to the king, "O Nebuchadnezzar, we do not need to defend ourselves before you in this matter. If we are thrown into the blazing furnace, the God we serve is able to save us from it, and he will rescue us from your hand, O king. But even if he does not, we want you to know, O king, that we will not serve your gods or worship the image of gold you have set up."

Then Nebuchadnezzar was furious with Shadrach, Meshach and Abednego, and his attitude toward them changed. He ordered the furnace heated seven times hotter than usual and commanded some of the strongest soldiers in his army to tie up Shadrach, Meshach and Abednego and throw them into the blazing furnace. So these men, wearing their robes, trousers, turbans and other clothes, were bound and thrown into the blazing furnace. The king's command was so urgent and the furnace so hot that the flames of the fire killed the soldiers who took up Shadrach, Meshach and Abednego, and these three men, firmly tied, fell into the blazing furnace.

Then King Nebuchadnezzar leaped to his feet in amazement and asked his advisers, "Weren't there three men that we tied up and threw into the fire?" They replied, "Certainly, O king."

He said, "Look! I see four men walking around in the fire, unbound and unharmed, and the fourth looks like a son of the gods."

Nebuchadnezzar then approached the opening of the blazing furnace and shouted, "Shadrach, Meshach and Abednego, servants of the Most High God, come out! Come here!" So Shadrach, Meshach and Abednego came out of the fire, and the satraps, prefects, governors and royal advisers crowded around them. They saw that the fire had not harmed their bodies, nor was a hair of their heads singed; their robes were not scorched, and there was no smell of fire on them.

DANIEL 3:16–27 NIV

But God didn't stop any of these things from happening. He let those problems happen, and every one of those persons was drawn closer to God as a result.

Problems also force us to look to God and to depend on him instead of ourselves.

We felt we were doomed to die and saw how powerless we were to help ourselves; but that was good, for then we put everything into the hands of God, who alone could save us.

2 CORINTHIANS 1:9 LB

Because God is sovereignly in control, accidents are just incidents in God's good plan for you.

We know that God causes everything to work together for the good of those who love God and are called according to his purpose for them. For God knew his people in advance, and he chose them to become like his Son.

ROMANS 8:28–29 NLT

Every problem is a character-building opportunity, and the more difficult it is, the greater the potential for building spiritual muscle and moral fiber.

We know that these troubles produce patience. And patience produces character.

ROMANS 5:3–4 NCV

———

Troubles come to prove that your faith is pure. This purity of faith is worth more than gold.

1 PETER 1:7 NCV

———

Under pressure, your faith-life is forced into the open and shows its true colors.

JAMES 1:3 THE MESSAGE

———

Since God intends to make you like Jesus, he will take you through the same experiences Jesus went through.

Although he was a son, he learned obedience from what he suffered and, once made perfect, he became the source of eternal salvation for all who obey him.

HEBREWS 5:8–9 NIV

———

We go through exactly what Christ goes through. If we go through the hard times with him, then we're certainly going to go through the good times with him!

ROMANS 8:17 THE MESSAGE

———

Problems don't automatically produce what God intends. Many people become bitter, rather than better, and never grow up. You have to respond the way Jesus would.

1. To deal with suffering as Jesus did, remember that God's plan is good.

"I know the plans I have for you," declares the LORD, "plans to prosper you and not to harm you, plans to give you hope and a future."

JEREMIAH 29:11 NIV

———

Joseph understood this truth when he told his brothers who had sold him into slavery,

"You intended to harm me, but God intended it for good."

GENESIS 50:20 NIV

———

Hezekiah echoed the same sentiment about his life-threatening illness:

"It was for my own good that I had such hard times."

ISAIAH 38:17 CEV

———

The secret of endurance is to remember that your pain is temporary but your reward will be eternal.

God is doing what is best for us, training us to live God's holy best.

HEBREWS 12:10 THE MESSAGE

Keep your eyes on Jesus, our leader and instructor. He was willing to die a shameful death on the cross because of the joy he knew would be his afterwards.

HEBREWS 12:2 LB

By faith Moses, when he had grown up, refused to be known as the son of Pharaoh's daughter. He chose to be mistreated along with the people of God rather than to enjoy the pleasures of sin for a short time. He regarded disgrace for the sake of Christ as of greater value than the treasures of Egypt, because he was looking ahead to his reward.

HEBREWS 11:24–26 NIV

Our present troubles are quite small and won't last very long. Yet they produce for us an immeasurably great glory that will last forever!

2 CORINTHIANS 4:17 NLT

If we are to share Christ's glory, we must also share his suffering. What we suffer now is nothing compared to the glory he will give us later.

ROMANS 8:17–18 NLT

Be full of joy [when you are persecuted], because you have a great reward waiting for you in heaven.

LUKE 6:23 NCV

---

2. To deal with suffering as Jesus did, we must rejoice and give thanks in the midst of it.

Give thanks in all circumstances, for this is God's will for you in Christ Jesus.

1 THESSALONIANS 5:18 NIV

Rejoice in the Lord always.

PHILIPPIANS 4:4 NIV

---

3. To deal with suffering as Jesus did, refuse to give up.

Let the process go on until your endurance is fully developed, and you will find that you have become men of mature character . . . with no weak spots.

JAMES 1:3–4 PH.

———

You need to stick it out, staying with God's plan so you'll be there for the promised completion.

HEBREWS 10:36 THE MESSAGE

———

REFLECTIONS

_____

_____

_____

_____

_____

_____

_____

_____

_____

_____

_____

_____

_____

_____

_____

_____

_____

_____

_____

Growing Through Temptation

Happy is the man who doesn't give in and do wrong when he is tempted, for afterwards he will get as his reward the crown of life that God has promised those who love him.

JAMES 1:12 LB

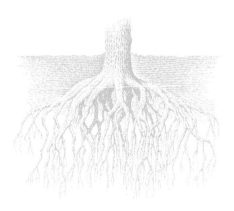

On the path to spiritual maturity, even temptation becomes a stepping-stone rather than a stumbling block when you realize that it is just as much an occasion to do the right thing as it is to do the wrong thing. Every time you choose to do good instead of sin, you are growing in the character of Christ:

When the Holy Spirit controls our lives, he will produce this kind of fruit in us: love, joy, peace, patience, kindness, goodness, faithfulness, gentleness, and self-control.

GALATIANS 5:22–23 NLT

God uses the opposite situation of each fruit to allow us a choice. Integrity is built by defeating the temptation to be dishonest; humility grows when we refuse to be prideful; and endurance develops every time you reject the temptation to give up. Every time you defeat a temptation, you become more like Jesus!

From the Bible we learn that temptation follows a four-step process. All temptations follow the same pattern. That's why Paul said,

We are very familiar with Satan's evil schemes.

2 CORINTHIANS 2:11 NLT

Step one, Satan identifies a desire *inside of you. Temptation always starts in your mind.*

Jesus said, "For from within, out of a person's heart, come evil thoughts, sexual immorality, theft, murder, adultery, greed, wickedness, deceit, eagerness for lustful pleasure, envy, slander, pride, and foolishness. All these vile things come from within."

MARK 7:21–23 NLT

[There is] a whole army of evil desires within you.

JAMES 4:1 LB

Step two is doubt. *Satan tries to get you to doubt what God has said about sin.*

Watch out! Don't let evil thoughts or doubts make any of you turn from the living God.

HEBREWS 3:12 CEV

Step three is deception. *Satan is incapable of telling the truth. He offers his lie to replace what God has already said in his Word.*

Jesus said, "The devil was a murderer from the beginning, not holding to the truth, for there is no truth in him. When he lies, he speaks his native language, for he is a liar and the father of lies."

JOHN 8:44 NIV

———

Step four is disobedience. *You finally act on the thought you've been toying with in your mind.*

We are tempted when we are drawn away and trapped by our own evil desires. Then our evil desires conceive and give birth to sin; and sin, when it is full-grown, gives birth to death. Do not be deceived, my dear friends!

JAMES 1:14–16 TEV

———

Understanding how temptation works is in itself helpful, but there are specific steps you need to take to overcome it.

1. Refuse to be intimidated. It is not a sin to be tempted. Jesus was tempted, yet he never sinned.

Remember that the temptations that come into your life are no different from what others experience.

1 CORINTHIANS 10:13 NLT

[Jesus] understands our weaknesses, for he faced all of the same temptations we do, yet he did not sin.

HEBREWS 4:15 NLT

2. *Recognize your pattern of temptation and be prepared for it.*

Stay alert. The Devil is poised to pounce, and would like nothing better than to catch you napping.

1 PETER 5:8 THE MESSAGE

Jesus said, "Watch and pray so that you will not fall into temptation. The spirit is willing, but the body is weak."

MATTHEW 26:41 NIV

Don't give the Devil a chance.

EPHESIANS 4:27 TEV

Put on the full armor of God so that you can take your stand against the devil's schemes.

EPHESIANS 6:11 NIV

Let us not be like others, who are asleep, but let us be alert and self-controlled.

1 THESSALONIANS 5:6 NIV

———

Prepare your minds for action; be self-controlled; set your hope fully on the grace to be given you when Jesus Christ is revealed.

1 PETER 1:13 NIV

———

Plan carefully what you do, and whatever you do will turn out right. Avoid evil and walk straight ahead. Don't go one step off the right way.

PROVERBS 4:26–27 TEV

———

God's people avoid evil ways,
    and they protect themselves by watching
        where they go.

PROVERBS 16:17 CEV

———

3. *Request God's help.*

"Call on me in times of trouble.
  I will rescue you, and you will honor me," says
    the Lord.

PSALM 50:15 GWT

―――

Let us have confidence, then, and approach God's
throne, where there is grace. There we will
receive mercy and find grace to help us just when
we need it.

HEBREWS 4:16 TEV

―――

**Instead of giving in or giving up, look up to
God, expect him to help you, and remember
the reward that is waiting for you:**

When people are tempted and still continue
strong, they should be happy. After they have
proved their faith, God will reward them with life
forever.

JAMES 1:12 NCV

―――

REFLECTIONS

_____

_____

_____

_____

_____

_____

_____

_____

_____

_____

_____

_____

_____

_____

_____

_____

_____

_____

_____

_____

_____

_____

Defeating Temptation

Run from anything that gives you the evil
thoughts that young men often have, but stay
close to anything that makes you want to do right.

2 TIMOTHY 2:22 LB

Remember that the temptations that come into
your life are no different from what others
experience. And God is faithful. He will keep the
temptation from becoming so strong that you
can't stand up against it. When you are tempted,
he will show you a way out so that you will not
give in to it.

1 CORINTHIANS 10:13 NLT

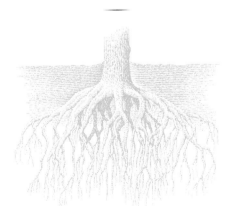

God has promised never to allow more on you than he puts *within* you to handle it. He will not permit any temptation that you could not overcome. However, you must do your part too by practicing four biblical keys to defeating temptation.

1. Refocus your attention on something else.

Keep me from paying attention to what is
    worthless, LORD.

PSALM 119:37 TEV

Do not be overcome by evil, but overcome evil with good.

ROMANS 12:21 NIV

Job said, "I made covenant with my eyes not to look with lust upon a young woman."

JOB 31:1 NLT

Always think about Jesus Christ.
2 TIMOTHY 2:8 GWT

Fill your minds with those things that are good
and that deserve praise: things that are true,
noble, right, pure, lovely, and honorable.
PHILIPPIANS 4:8 TEV

Be careful how you think; your life is shaped by
your thoughts.
PROVERBS 4:23 TEV

We capture every thought and make it give up
and obey Christ.
2 CORINTHIANS 10:5 NCV

Fix your thoughts on Jesus.
HEBREWS 3:1 NIV

2. *Reveal your struggle to a godly friend or support group.*

You are better off to have a friend than to be all alone. . . . If you fall, your friend can help you up. But if you fall without having a friend nearby, you are really in trouble.

ECCLESIASTES 4:9–10 CEV

———

Confess your sins to each other and pray for each other so that you may be healed.

JAMES 5:16 NIV

———

Yes, it is humbling to admit our weaknesses to others, but lack of humility is the very thing that is keeping you from getting better.

As the Scriptures say,
  "God sets himself against the proud,
      but he shows favor to the humble."
So humble yourselves before God.

JAMES 4:6–7 NLT

———

3. *Resist the Devil.*

Resist the devil and he will flee from you.

JAMES 4:7 NIV

———

Put on salvation as your helmet, and take the sword of the Spirit, which is the word of God.

EPHESIANS 6:17 NLT

———

4. *Realize your vulnerability.*

The heart is deceitful above all things
    and beyond cure.

JEREMIAH 17:9 NIV

———

Don't be so naive and self-confident. You're not exempt. You could fall flat on your face as easily as anyone else. Forget about self-confidence; it's useless. Cultivate God-confidence.

1 CORINTHIANS 10:12 THE MESSAGE

———

REFLECTIONS

_____

_____

_____

_____

_____

_____

_____

_____

_____

_____

_____

_____

_____

_____

_____

_____

_____

_____

_____

It Takes Time

Everything on earth has its own time and its own season.

ECCLESIASTES 3:1 CEV

I am sure that God who began the good work within you will keep right on helping you grow in his grace until his task within you is finally finished on that day when Jesus Christ returns.

PHILIPPIANS 1:6 LB

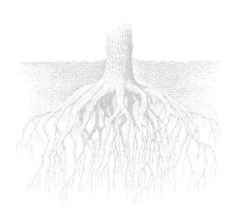

Discipleship is the process of conforming to Christ. Christlikeness is your eventual destination, but your journey will last a lifetime. There are no shortcuts to maturity.

We arrive at real maturity—that measure of development which is meant by "the fullness of Christ."

EPHESIANS 4:13 PH.

You have begun to live the new life, in which you are being made new and are becoming like the One who made you.

COLOSSIANS 3:10 NCV

Our lives gradually become brighter and more beautiful as God enters our lives and we become like him.

2 CORINTHIANS 3:18 THE MESSAGE

Although God *could* instantly transform us, he has chosen to develop us slowly. Why does it take so long to change and grow up?

You were taught, with regard to your former way of life, to put off your old self, which is being corrupted by its deceitful desires; to be made new in the attitude of your minds; and to put on the new self, created to be like God in true righteousness and holiness.

EPHESIANS 4:22–24 NIV

Now you must rid yourselves of all such things as these: anger, rage, malice, slander, and filthy language from your lips. Do not lie to each other, since you have taken off your old self with its practices and have put on the new self, which is being renewed in knowledge in the image of its Creator.

COLOSSIANS 3:8–10 NIV

Practice [spiritual disciplines]. Devote your life to them so that everyone can see your progress.

1 TIMOTHY 4:15 GWT

As you grow to spiritual maturity, there are several ways to cooperate with God in the process.

1. Believe God is working in your life even when you don't feel it.

God began doing a good work in you, and I am sure he will continue it until it is finished when Jesus Christ comes again.

PHILIPPIANS 1:6 NCV

Everything on earth has its own time and its own season.

ECCLESIASTES 3:1 CEV

---

2. Keep a notebook or journal of lessons learned.

It's crucial that we keep a firm grip on what we've heard so that we don't drift off.

HEBREWS 2:1 THE MESSAGE

---

3. Be patient with God and with yourself.

Don't try to get out of anything prematurely. Let it do its work so you become mature and well-developed.

JAMES 1:4 THE MESSAGE

———

"These things I plan won't happen right away. Slowly, steadily, surely, the time approaches when the vision will be fulfilled. If it seems slow, do not despair, for these things will surely come to pass. Just be patient! They will not be overdue a single day!" says the Lord.

HABAKKUK 2:3 LB

———

God who began a good work in you will carry it on to completion.

PHILIPPIANS 1:6 NIV

———

REFLECTIONS

DAILY INSPIRATION FOR THE PURPOSE-DRIVEN LIFE

REFLECTIONS

_____

_____

_____

_____

_____

_____

_____

_____

_____

_____

_____

_____

_____

_____

_____

_____

_____

_____

_____

_____

_____

Purpose 4:

YOU WERE SHAPED FOR SERVING GOD

❧

Who is Apollos? And who is Paul? We are simply God's servants, by whom you were led to believe. Each one of us does the work which the Lord gave him to do: I planted the seed, Apollos watered the plant, but it was God who made the plant grow.

1 CORINTHIANS 3:5–6 TEV

Accepting Your Assignment

It is God himself who has made us what we are and given us new lives from Christ Jesus; and long ages ago he planned that we should spend these lives helping others.

EPHESIANS 2:10 LB

Jesus prayed, "I glorified you, Father, on earth by completing down to the last detail what you assigned me to do."

JOHN 17:4 THE MESSAGE

You were created to serve God. You were placed on this planet for a special assignment.

God has created us for a life of good deeds, which he has already prepared for us to do.
EPHESIANS 2:10 TEV

———

Serve wholeheartedly, as if you were serving the Lord, not men, because you know that the Lord will reward everyone for whatever good he does.
EPHESIANS 6:7–8 NIV

———

"Before I made you in your mother's womb,
    I chose you.
Before you were born, I set you apart for a
    special work," says the Lord.
JEREMIAH 1:5 NCV

———

You were saved to serve God. You're not saved *by* service, but you are saved *for* service.

It is God who saved us and chose us for his holy work, not because we deserved it but because that was his plan.

2 TIMOTHY 1:9 LB

God paid a great price for you. So use your body to honor God.

1 CORINTHIANS 6:20 CEV

Because of God's great mercy to us I appeal to you: Offer yourselves as a living sacrifice to God, dedicated to his service and pleasing to him.

ROMANS 12:1 TEV

Our love for each other proves that we have gone from death to life.

1 JOHN 3:14 CEV

When Peter's sick mother-in-law was healed by Jesus, she instantly "stood up and began to serve Jesus" using her new gift of health. We are healed to help others (1 Corinthians 12:29–30).

You are called to serve God. Regardless of your job or career, you are called to *full-time* Christian service.

Those God foreknew he also predestined to be conformed to the likeness of his Son, that he might be the firstborn among many brothers. And those he predestined, he also called; those he called, he also justified; those he justified, he also glorified.
ROMANS 8:29–30 NIV

———

God saved us and called us to be his own people, not because of what we have done, but because of his own purpose.
2 TIMOTHY 1:9 TEV

———

You were chosen to tell about the excellent qualities of God, who called you.
1 PETER 2:9 GWT

———

Now you belong to him who was raised from the dead in order that we might be useful in the service of God.
ROMANS 7:4 TEV

———

All of you together [in the church] are Christ's body, and each one of you is a separate and necessary part of it.

1 Corinthians 12:27 NLT

You are commanded to serve God. Jesus came "to serve" and "to give"—and those two verbs should define your life on earth, too.

Jesus said, "Your attitude must be like my own, for I, the Messiah, did not come to be served, but to serve and to give my life."

Matthew 20:28 LB

One day God will compare how much time and energy we spent on ourselves compared with what we invested in serving others.

Remember, each of us will stand personally before the judgment seat of God. . . . Yes, each of us will have to give a personal account to God.

Romans 14:10, 12

Jesus said, "If you insist on saving your life, you will lose it. Only those who throw away their lives for my sake and for the sake of the Good News will ever know what it means to really live."

Mark 8:35 LB

God will pour out his anger and wrath on those
who live for themselves.

ROMANS 2:8 NLT

———

**Service is the pathway to real significance. It
is through ministry that we discover the
meaning of our lives.**

Each of us finds our meaning and function as a
part of Christ's body.

ROMANS 12:5 THE MESSAGE

———

I want you to think about how all this makes you
more significant, not less . . . because of what you
are a part of.

1 CORINTHIANS 12:14, 19 THE MESSAGE

———

We are God's workmanship, created in Christ
Jesus to do good works, which God prepared in
advance for us to do.

EPHESIANS 2:10 NIV

———

REFLECTIONS

Shaped for Serving God

Your hands shaped me and made me, LORD.
JOB 10:8 NIV

"The people I have shaped for myself
Will broadcast my praises," says the LORD.
ISAIAH 43:21 NJB

Each of us was uniquely designed, or "*shaped*," to do certain things. You are the way you are because you were made for a specific ministry.

You made all the delicate, inner parts of my body
    and knit me together in my mother's womb.
Thank you for making me so wonderfully
        complex!
    Your workmanship is marvelous, Lord.

PSALM 139:13–14 NLT

———

Every day of my life was recorded in your
        book, LORD.
    Every moment was laid out before a single day
        had passed.

PSALM 139:16 NLT

———

We are God's workmanship, created in Christ
Jesus to do good works.

EPHESIANS 2:10 NIV

———

Whenever God gives us an assignment, he always equips us with what we need to accomplish it. This custom combination of capabilities is called your SHAPE.

Spiritual gifts

Heart

Abilities

Personality

Experience

SPIRITUAL GIFTS: These are special God-empowered abilities for serving him that are given only to believers.

Whoever does not have the Spirit cannot receive the gifts that come from God's Spirit.

1 CORINTHIANS 2:14 TEV

———

Just as each of us has one body with many members, and these members do not all have the same function, so in Christ we who are many form one body, and each member belongs to all the others. We have different gifts, according to the grace given us. If a man's gift is prophesying, let him use it in proportion to his faith. If it is serving, let him serve; if it is teaching, let him teach; if it is encouraging, let him encourage; if it is contributing to the needs of others, let him give generously; if it is leadership, let him govern diligently; if it is showing mercy, let him do it cheerfully.

ROMANS 12:4–8 NIV

———

It was God who gave some to be apostles, some to be prophets, some to be evangelists, and some to be pastors and teachers, to prepare God's people for works of service, so that the body of Christ may be built up.

EPHESIANS 4:11–12 NIV

———

Each man has his own gift from God; one has this gift, another has that.

1 Corinthians 7:7 niv

———

Christ has generously divided out his gifts to us.

Ephesians 4:7 cev

———

It is the one and only Holy Spirit who distributes these gifts. He alone decides which gift each person should have.

1 Corinthians 12:11 nlt

———

A spiritual gift is given to each of us as a means of helping the entire church.

1 Corinthians 12:7 nlt

———

There are different kinds of service in the church, but it is the same Lord we are serving.

1 Corinthians 12:5 nlt

———

Heart: Your heart represents the source of all your motivations—what you love to do and what you care about most. Another word for heart is *passion*. Don't ignore your interests. Consider how they might be used for God's glory. There is a reason that you love to do these things.

As a face is reflected in water,
  so the heart reflects the person.
                    PROVERBS 27:19 NLT

———

Serve the LORD with all your heart.
                    1 SAMUEL 12:20 NIV

———

Above all else, guard your heart,
  for it is the wellspring of life.
                    PROVERBS 4:23 NIV

———

A simple life in the fear-of-God is better than a rich
  life with a ton of headaches.
                    PROVERBS 15:16 THE MESSAGE

———

REFLECTIONS

Understanding Your Shape

You shaped me first inside, then out, LORD;
you formed me in my mother's womb.

PSALM 139:13 THE MESSAGE

ABILITIES: Your abilities are the natural talents you were born with.

All our abilities come from God.

God has given each of us the ability to do certain things well.

ROMANS 12:6 NLT

Every ability can be used for God's glory.

Whatever you do, do it all for the glory of God.

1 CORINTHIANS 10:31 NIV

There are different kinds of spiritual gifts ... different ways of serving ... [and] different abilities to perform service.

1 CORINTHIANS 12:4–6 TEV

Remember the Lord your God, for it is he who gives you the ability to produce wealth.

DEUTERONOMY 8:18 NIV

[God provided the Temple craftsmen with] skill, ability, and knowledge in all kinds of crafts to make artistic designs ... and to engage in all kinds of craftsmanship.

EXODUS 31:3–5 NIV

What you're *able* to do, God *wants* you to do. No one else can play your role, because they don't have the unique shape that God has given you.

God has given each of you some special abilities; be sure to use them to help each other, passing on to others God's many kinds of blessings.

1 PETER 4:10 LB

———

[God equips you] with all you need for doing his will.

HEBREWS 13:21 LB

———

PERSONALITY: God created each of us with a unique combination of personality traits. There is no "right" or "wrong" temperament for ministry. We need all kinds of personalities to balance the church and give it flavor.

God works through different people in different ways, but it is the same God who achieves his purpose through them all.

1 CORINTHIANS 12:6 PH.

———

EXPERIENCES: You have been shaped by your experiences in life, most of which were beyond your control. God allowed them for his purpose of molding you.

God comforts us in all our troubles so that we can comfort others. When other are troubled, we will be able to give them the same comfort God has given us.

2 CORINTHIANS 1:4 NLT

———

Paul understood this truth, so he was honest about his bouts with depression:

I think you ought to know, dear brothers, about the hard time we went through in Asia. We were really crushed and overwhelmed, and feared we would never live through it. We felt we were doomed to die and saw how powerless we were to help ourselves; but that was good, for then we put everything into the hands of God, who alone could save us, for he can even raise the dead. And he did help us and saved us from a terrible death; yes, and we expect him to do it again and again.

2 CORINTHIANS 1:8–10 LB

———

REFLECTIONS

_____

_____

_____

_____

_____

_____

_____

_____

_____

_____

_____

_____

_____

_____

_____

_____

_____

_____

_____

Using What God Gave You

Since we find ourselves fashioned into all these excellently formed and marvelously functioning parts in Christ's body, let's just go ahead and be what we were made to be.

ROMANS 12:5 THE MESSAGE

Discover your shape: Begin by assessing your gifts and abilities.

Don't act thoughtlessly, but try to find out and do whatever the Lord wants you to.

EPHESIANS 5:17 LB

———

Try to have a sane estimate of your capabilities.

ROMANS 12:3 PH

———

Consider your heart and your personality.

Make a careful exploration of who you are and the work you have been given, and then sink yourself into that.

GALATIANS 6:4 THE MESSAGE

———

Examine your experiences and extract the lessons you have learned.

Remember today what you have learned about the LORD through your experiences with him.

DEUTERONOMY 11:2 TEV

———

When Jesus washed Peter's feet, he said,

"You do not realize now what I am doing, but later you will understand."

JOHN 13:7 NIV

Only in hindsight do we understand how God intended a problem for good.

Were all your experiences wasted? I hope not!

GALATIANS 3:4 NCV

Since God knows what's best for you, you should gratefully accept the way he fashioned you.

What right have you, a human being, to cross-examine God? The pot has no right to say to the potter: "Why did you make me this shape?" Surely a potter can do what he likes with the clay!

ROMANS 9:20–21 LB

Christ has given each of us special abilities—whatever he wants us to have out of his rich storehouse of gifts.

EPHESIANS 4:7 LB

Part of accepting your shape is recognizing your limitations. God assigns each of us a field or sphere of service.

Our goal is to stay within the boundaries of God's plan for us.

2 CORINTHIANS 10:13 NLT

———

[We must] run with patience the particular race that God has set before us.

HEBREWS 12:1 LB

———

Do your best to present yourself to God as one approved, a workman who does not need to be ashamed and who correctly handles the word of truth.

2 TIMOTHY 2:15 NIV

———

Be sure to do what you should, for then you will enjoy the personal satisfaction of having done your work well, and you won't need to compare yourself to anyone else.

GALATIANS 6:4 NLT

———

We do not dare to classify or compare ourselves with some who commend themselves. When they measure themselves by themselves and compare themselves with themselves, they are not wise.

2 CORINTHIANS 10:12 NIV

———

In all this comparing and grading and competing, they quite miss the point.

2 CORINTHIANS 10:12 THE MESSAGE

Keep developing your shape. We are to cultivate our gifts and abilities, keep our hearts aflame, grow our character and personality, and broaden our experiences so we will be increasingly more effective in our service.

Keep on growing in your knowledge and understanding.

PHILIPPIANS 1:9 NLT

———

Do your own work well, and then you will have something to be proud of. But don't compare yourself with others.

GALATIANS 6:4 CEV

———

Kindle afresh the gift of God which is in you.

2 TIMOTHY 1:6 NASB

———

Be sure to use the abilities God has given you. . . .
Put these abilities to work; throw yourself into
your tasks so that everyone may notice your
improvement and progress.

1 TIMOTHY 4:14–15 LB

**In Jesus' parable of the talents, the master
said to the servant who had failed to use his
one talent:**

Take the talent from him and give it to the one
who has ten talents.

MATTHEW 25:28 NIV

**Fail to use what you've been given and you'll
lose it.**

Concentrate on doing your best for God, work
you won't be ashamed of.

2 TIMOTHY 2:15 THE MESSAGE

Like athletes preparing for the Olympics, we keep
training for that big day:
They do it for a gold medal that tarnishes and
fades. You're after one that's gold eternally.

1 CORINTHIANS 9:25 THE MESSAGE

REFLECTIONS

_____

_____

_____

_____

_____

_____

_____

_____

_____

_____

_____

_____

_____

_____

_____

_____

_____

_____

_____

How Real Servants Act

Jesus said, "Whoever wants to be great must become a servant."

MARK 10:43 THE MESSAGE

You can tell what they are by what they do.
MATTHEW 7:16 CEV

We serve God by serving others. How can you know if you have the heart of a servant?

Real servants make themselves available to serve.

No soldier in active service entangles himself in the affairs of everyday life, so that he may please the one who enlisted him.

2 TIMOTHY 2:4 NASB

———

If you think you are too important to help someone in need, you are only fooling yourself. You are really a nobody.

GALATIANS 6:3 NLT

———

Being a servant means giving up the right to control your schedule and allowing God to interrupt it whenever he needs to.

Real servants pay attention to needs.

Whenever we have the opportunity, we have to do what is good for everyone, especially for the family of believers.

GALATIANS 6:10 GWT

———

Never tell your neighbors to wait until tomorrow
  if you can help them now.

PROVERBS 3:28 TEV

———

Real servants do their best with what they have.

If you wait for perfect conditions, you will never get anything done.

ECCLESIASTES 11:4 NLT

———

Real servants do every task with equal dedication.

Jesus said, "You call me 'Teacher' and 'Lord,' and rightly so, for that is what I am. Now that I, your Lord and Teacher, have washed your feet, you also should wash one another's feet. I have set you an example that you should do as I have done for you. I tell you the truth, no servant is greater than his master, nor is a messenger greater than the one who sent him. Now that you know these things, you will be blessed if you do them."

JOHN 13:13–17 NIV

———

Jesus said, "Whoever can be trusted with very little can also be trusted with much."

LUKE 16:10 NIV

———

Real servants are faithful to their ministry.

Imagine what it will feel like one day to have God say to you,

"Well done, my good and faithful servant. You have been faithful in handling this small amount, so now I will give you many more responsibilities. Let's celebrate together!"

MATTHEW 25:23 NLT

Real servants maintain a low profile.

Put on the apron of humility, to serve one another.

1 PETER 5:5 TEV

Jesus said, "When you do good deeds, don't try to show off. If you do, you won't get a reward from your Father in heaven."

MATTHEW 6:1 CEV

If I were still trying to please men, I would not be a servant of Christ.

GALATIANS 1:10 NIV

When Christ (your real life, remember) shows up
again on this earth, you'll show up, too—the real
you, the glorious you. Meanwhile, be content with
obscurity.

COLOSSIANS 3:4 THE MESSAGE

———

Throw yourselves into the work of the Master,
confident that nothing you do for him is a waste
of time or effort.

1 CORINTHIANS 15:58 THE MESSAGE

———

Jesus said, "If, as my representatives, you give
even a cup of cold water to a little child, you will
surely be rewarded."

MATTHEW 10:42 LB

———

REFLECTIONS

_____

_____

_____

_____

_____

_____

_____

_____

_____

_____

_____

_____

_____

_____

_____

_____

_____

_____

_____

Thinking Like a Servant

Think of yourselves the way Christ Jesus thought of himself.

PHILIPPIANS 2:5 THE MESSAGE

My servant Caleb thinks differently and follows me completely.

NUMBERS 14:24 NCV

DAILY INSPIRATION FOR THE PURPOSE-DRIVEN LIFE

Servants think more about others than about themselves. It's only when we forget ourselves that we do the things that deserve to be remembered.

Forget yourselves long enough to lend a helping hand.

PHILIPPIANS 2:4 THE MESSAGE

———

[Jesus] emptied himself by taking on the form of a servant.

PHILIPPIANS 2:7 GWT

———

Jesus said, "If someone takes unfair advantage of you, use the occasion to practice the servant life."

MATTHEW 5:41 THE MESSAGE

———

**Servants think like stewards, not owners.
Servants remember that God owns it all.**

The one thing required of such servants is that
they be faithful to their master.

1 CORINTHIANS 4:2 TEV

———

Jesus said, "No servant can serve two masters.
Either he will hate the one and love the other, or
he will be devoted to the one and despise the
other. You cannot serve both God and Money."

LUKE 16:13 NIV

———

Jesus said, "If you have not been trustworthy in
handling worldly wealth, who will trust you with
true riches?"

LUKE 16:11 NIV

———

King Amaziah lost God's favor because:

He did what was right in the sight of the Lord,
yet not with a true heart.

2 CHRONICLES 25:2 NRSV

———

Servants think about their work, not what others are doing. They don't compare, criticize, or compete with other servants or ministries. They're too busy doing the work God has given them.

We will not compare ourselves with each other as if one of us were better and another worse. We have far more interesting things to do with our lives. Each of us is an original.

GALATIANS 5:26 THE MESSAGE

———

[Nehemiah said to those who were trying to distract him as he worked to rebuild the temple], "My work is too important to stop now and . . . visit with you."

NEHEMIAH 6:3 CEV

———

Who are you to criticize someone else's servant? The Lord will determine whether his servant has been successful.

ROMANS 14:4 GWT

———

When Jesus was at Bethany, a guest of Simon the Leper, a woman came up to him as he was eating dinner and anointed him with a bottle of very expensive perfume. When the disciples saw what was happening, they were furious. "That's criminal! This could have been sold for a lot and the money handed out to the poor." When Jesus realized what was going on, he intervened. "Why are you giving this woman a hard time? She has just done something wonderfully significant for me. You will have the poor with you every day for the rest of your lives, but not me. When she poured this perfume on my body, what she really did was anoint me for burial. You can be sure that wherever in the whole world the Message is preached, what she has just done is going to be remembered and admired."

JOHN 13:6–13 THE MESSAGE

Servants base their identity in Christ. Because they remember they are loved and accepted by grace, servants don't have to prove their worth.

Washing feet was the equivalent of being a shoeshine boy, a job devoid of status. But Jesus knew who he was, so the task didn't threaten his self-image.

Jesus knew that the Father had put all things under his power, and that he had come from God and was returning to God; so he got up from the meal, took off his outer clothing, and wrapped a towel around his waist. After that, he poured water into a basin and began to wash his disciples' feet, drying them with the towel that was wrapped around him.

JOHN 13:3–5 NIV

You may brag about yourself, but the only approval that counts is the Lord's approval.

2 CORINTHIANS 10:18 CEV

James had the credentials of growing up with Jesus as his brother. Yet, in introducing his letter, he simply referred to himself as:

A servant of God and of the Lord Jesus Christ.

JAMES 1:1

Servants think of ministry as an opportunity, not an obligation.

Serve the LORD with gladness.

PSALM 100:2 KJV

Jesus said, "The Father will honor and reward anyone who serves me."

JOHN 12:26 THE MESSAGE

God will not forget how hard you have worked for him and how you have shown your love to him by caring for other Christians.

HEBREWS 6:10 NLT

REFLECTIONS

_____

_____

_____

_____

_____

_____

_____

_____

_____

_____

_____

_____

_____

_____

_____

_____

_____

_____

_____

_____

God's Power in Your Weakness

To be sure, [Jesus] was crucified in weakness, yet
he lives by God's power. Likewise, we are weak in
him, yet by God's power we will live with him to
serve you.

2 Corinthians 13:4 niv

Jesus said, "I am with you; that is all you need.
My power shows up best in weak people."

2 Corinthians 12:9 lb

God loves to use weak people. Usually we deny our weaknesses, defend them, excuse them, hide them, and resent them. This prevents God from using them the way he desires. God has a different perspective on your weaknesses.

"My thoughts and my ways are higher than
    yours," says the LORD.

ISAIAH 55:9 CEV

———

God purposely chose what the world considers nonsense in order to shame the wise, and he chose what the world considers weak in order to shame the powerful.

1 CORINTHIANS 1:27 TEV

———

We are like clay jars in which this treasure [of the gospel] is stored. The real power comes from God and not from us.

2 CORINTHIANS 4:7 CEV

———

God will use us if we allow him to work through our weaknesses.

1. Admit your weaknesses.

Peter said to Jesus,

You are the Christ, the Son of the living God.
MATTHEW 16:16 NIV

———

Paul said to an idolizing crowd,

We are only human beings like you.
ACTS 14:15 NCV

———

If you want God to use you, you must know who God is and know who you are.

2. Be content with your weaknesses.

I am glad to boast about my weaknesses, so that the power of Christ may work through me. Since I know it is all for Christ's good, I am quite content with my weaknesses.

2 CORINTHIANS 12:9–10 NLT

———

When I am weak, then I am strong—the less I have, the more I depend on Christ.

2 CORINTHIANS 12:10 LB

———

So I wouldn't get a big head, I was given the gift of a handicap to keep me in constant touch with my limitations.

2 CORINTHIANS 12:7 THE MESSAGE

———

I am quite happy about [my weakness] . . . for when I am weak, then I am strong—the less I have, the more I depend on him.

2 CORINTHIANS 12:10 LB

———

The great missionary Hudson Taylor said, "All God's giants were weak people."

- Moses' weakness was his temper. Yet God transformed him into "*the humblest man on earth*" (Numbers 12:3).
- Gideon's weakness was low self-esteem and deep insecurities, but God transformed him into a "*mighty man of valor*" (Judges 6:12 KJV).
- Not once, but twice, Abraham claimed his wife was his sister to protect himself. But God transformed Abraham into "*the father of those who have faith*" (Romans 4:11 NLT).
- Impulsive, weak-willed Peter became "*a rock*" (Matthew 16:18 TEV).
- The adulterer David became "*a man after God's own heart*" (Acts 13:22 NLT).
- God specializes in turning weaknesses into strengths.
- The list could go on and on. "*It would take to long to recount the stories of the faith of … Barak, Samson, Jephthah, David, Samuel, and all the prophets. … Their weakness was turned into strength*" (Hebrews 11:32–34 NLT).

3. *Honestly share your weaknesses.*

[The apostle] Paul modeled vulnerability in all his letters. He openly shared his failures, feelings, frustrations, and fears.

When I want to do good, I don't, and when I try not to do wrong, I do it anyway.

ROMANS 7:19 NLT

———

I have told you all my feelings.

2 CORINTHIANS 6:11 LB

———

We were crushed and completely overwhelmed, and we thought we would never live through it.

2 CORINTHIANS 1:8 NLT

———

When I came to you, I was weak and fearful and trembling.

1 CORINTHIANS 2:3 NCV

———

Vulnerability is risky. But the benefits are worth the risk.

God gives grace to the humble.

JAMES 4:6 NIV

———

4. Glory in your weaknesses. Instead of posing as self-confident and invincible, see yourself as a trophy of grace.

I am going to boast only about how weak I am and how great God is to use such weaknesses for his glory.

2 CORINTHIANS 12:5 LB

The Spirit helps us in our weakness.

ROMANS 8:26 NIV

[Jesus] understands every weakness of ours.

HEBREWS 4:1 CEV

Jesus said, "My grace is sufficient for you, my power is made perfect in weakness."

2 CORINTHIANS 12:9 NIV

REFLECTIONS

_____

_____

_____

_____

_____

_____

_____

_____

_____

_____

_____

_____

_____

_____

_____

_____

_____

_____

_____

_____

DAILY INSPIRATION FOR THE PURPOSE-DRIVEN LIFE

Purpose 5:

YOU WERE MADE
FOR A MISSION

—— ❧ ——

The fruit of the righteous is a tree of life,
and he who wins souls is wise.
PROVERBS 11:30 NIV

Made for a Mission

Jesus said, "In the same way that you, Father, gave me a mission in the world, I give them [my followers] a mission in the world."

JOHN 17:18 THE MESSAGE

The most important thing is that I complete my mission, the work that the Lord Jesus gave me.

ACTS 20:24 NCV

Jesus clearly understood his life mission on earth. At age twelve he said,

I must be about my Father's business.
LUKE 2:49 KJV

———

Twenty-one years later, dying on the cross, he said,

It is finished.
JOHN 19:30

———

God is at work in the world, and he wants you to join him. Being a Christian includes being *sent* into the world as a representative of Jesus Christ.

Jesus said, "As the Father has sent me, I am sending you."
JOHN 20:21 NIV

———

Christ changed us from enemies into his friends and gave us the task of making others his friends also.
2 CORINTHIANS 5:18 TEV

———

We have been sent to speak for Christ.
2 CORINTHIANS 5:20 NCV

———

**Your mission is a continuation of Jesus'
mission on earth. As his followers, we are to
continue what Jesus started.**

Jesus said, "Go to the people of all nations and
make them my disciples. Baptize them in the
name of the Father, the Son, and the Holy Spirit,
and teach them to do everything I have told you."

MATTHEW 28:19–20 CEV

"You must warn [unbelievers] so they may live. If
you don't speak out to warn the wicked to stop
their evil ways, they will die in their sin," says the
LORD.

EZEKIEL 3:18 NCV

**You are the only Christian some people will
ever know, and your mission is to share Jesus
with them.**

Your mission is a wonderful privilege. Although it is a big responsibility, it is also an incredible honor to be used by God.

God has given us the privilege of urging everyone to come into his favor and be reconciled to him.

2 CORINTHIANS 5:18 LB

———

We are workers together with God.

2 CORINTHIANS 6:1 NCV

———

We're Christ's representatives. God uses us to persuade men and women to drop their differences and enter into God's work of making things right between them. We're speaking for Christ himself now: Become friends with God.

2 CORINTHIANS 5:20 THE MESSAGE

———

Telling others how they can have eternal life is the greatest thing you can do for them. Everybody needs Jesus.

Jesus is the only One who can save people.

ACTS 4:12 NCV

———

Your mission has eternal significance. Nothing else you do will ever matter as much as helping people establish an eternal relationship with God.

Jesus said, "All of us must quickly carry out the tasks assigned us by the one who sent me, because there is little time left before the night falls and all work comes to an end."

JOHN 9:4 NLT

———

Your mission gives your life meaning.

My life is worth nothing unless I use it for doing the work assigned me by the Lord Jesus—the work of telling others the Good News about God's wonderful kindness and love.

ACTS 20:24 NLT

———

God's timetable for history's conclusion is connected to the completion of our commission. Jesus will not return until everyone God wants to hear the Good News has heard it.

Jesus said, "No one knows about that day or hour [of my return], not even the angels in heaven, nor the Son, but only the Father."

MATTHEW 24:36 NIV

———

Jesus said, "It is not for you to know the times or dates the Father has set by his own authority. But you will receive power when the Holy Spirit comes on you; and you will be my witnesses in Jerusalem, and in all Judea and Samaria, and to the ends of the earth."

ACTS 1:7–8 NIV

———

Jesus said, "The Good News about God's kingdom will be preached in all the world, to every nation. Then the end will come."

MATTHEW 24:14 NCV

———

To fulfill your mission will require that you abandon your agenda and accept God's agenda for your life. You must say, like Jesus, "Father, . . . I want your will, not mine" (Luke 22:42 NLT).

Anyone who lets himself be distracted from the work I plan for him is not fit for the Kingdom of God.

LUKE 9:62 LB

———

Give yourselves completely to God—every part of you for you are back from death and you want to be tools in the hands of God, to be used for his good purposes.

ROMANS 6:13 LB

———

Jesus said, "God will give you all you need from day to day if you live for him and make the Kingdom of God your primary concern."

MATTHEW 6:33 NLT

———

If you want to be used by God, you must care about what God cares about; what he cares about most is the redemption of the people he made. He wants his lost children found!

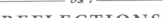

REFLECTIONS

_____

_____

_____

_____

_____

_____

_____

_____

_____

_____

_____

_____

_____

_____

_____

_____

_____

_____

_____

_____

_____

_____

Sharing Your Life Message

———— ✌ ————

Those who believe in the Son of God have the
testimony of God in them.

1 JOHN 5:10 GWT

————

God has given you a Life Message to share. God wants to speak to the world through you.

Your lives are echoing the Master's Word. . . . The news of your faith in God is out. We don't even have to say anything anymore—you're the message!

1 THESSALONIANS 1:8 THE MESSAGE

We speak the truth before God, as messengers of God.

2 CORINTHIANS 2:17 NCV

Jesus said, "You will be my witnesses."

ACTS 1:8 NIV

**Your Life Message includes your testimony—
the story of how Christ has made a difference
in your life.**

You are the ones chosen by God, chosen for the
high calling of priestly work, chosen to be a holy
people, God's instruments to do his work and
speak out for him, to tell others of the night-and-
day difference he made for you—from nothing to
something, from rejected to accepted.

1 Peter 2:9–10 The Message

Be ready at all times to answer anyone who asks
you to explain the hope you have in you, but do it
with gentleness and respect.

1 Peter 3:15–16 tev

Your Life Message includes your life lessons— the truths that God has taught you from experiences with him.

God, teach me lessons for living
    so I can stay the course.
        PSALM 119:33 THE MESSAGE

———

Sadly, we never learn from a lot that happens to us. Of the Israelites, the Bible says:

Over and over God rescued them, but they never learned—until finally their sins destroyed them.
        PSALM 106:43 THE MESSAGE

———

A warning given by an experienced person to someone willing to listen is more valuable than gold rings or jewelry made of the finest gold.

        PROVERBS 25:12 TEV

———

Your Life Message includes sharing your godly passions. As you grow closer to God, he will give you a passion for something he cares about deeply so you can be a spokesman for him in the world.

Jesus said, "A man's heart determines his speech."

MATTHEW 12:34 LB

———

My zeal for God and his work burns hot within me.

PSALM 69:9 LB

———

Your message burns in my heart and bones, and I cannot keep silent, LORD.

JEREMIAH 20:9 CEV

———

It is fine to be zealous, provided the purpose is good.

GALATIANS 4:18 NIV

———

Your Life Message includes the Good News— that when we trust God's grace to save us through what Jesus did, our sins are forgiven, we get a purpose for living, and we are promised a future home in heaven.

The Good News shows how God makes people right with himself—that it begins and ends with faith.

ROMANS 1:17 NCV

———

God was in Christ, reconciling the world to himself, no longer counting people's sins against them. This is the wonderful message he has given us to tell others.

2 CORINTHIANS 5:19 NLT

———

Christ's love compels us, because we are convinced that one died for all.

2 CORINTHIANS 5:14 NIV

———

**If you've been afraid to share the Good News
with those around you, ask God to fill your
heart with his love for them.**

There is no fear in love; perfect love drives out all
fear.

1 JOHN 4:18 TEV

———

[God] does not want anyone to be lost, but he
wants all people to change their hearts and lives.

2 PETER 3:9 NCV

———

Make the most of your chances to tell others the
Good News. Be wise in all your contacts with
them.

COLOSSIANS 4:5 LB

———

**Is anyone going to be in heaven because of
you? Imagine the joy of greeting people in
heaven whom you helped get there.**

REFLECTIONS

_____

_____

_____

_____

_____

_____

_____

_____

_____

_____

_____

_____

_____

_____

_____

_____

_____

_____

_____

Becoming a World-Class Christian

———— ✻ ————

Jesus said to his followers, "Go everywhere in the world, and tell the Good News to everyone."

MARK 16:15 NCV

————

Send us around the world with the news of your saving power, LORD, and your eternal plan for all mankind.

PSALM 67:2 LB

————

God invites you to participate in the greatest, largest, most diverse, and most significant cause in history—his kingdom. Nothing matters more. So, how do you think like a world-class Christian?

1. Shift from self-centered thinking to other-centered thinking.

My friends, stop thinking like children. Think like mature people.

1 CORINTHIANS 14:20 CEV

———

Don't think only about your own affairs, but be interested in others, too.

PHILIPPIANS 2:4 NLT

———

God has given us his Spirit. That's why we don't think the same way that the people of this world think.

1 CORINTHIANS 2:12 CEV

———

I don't think about what would be good for me but about what would be good for many people so that they might be saved.

1 CORINTHIANS 10:33 GWT

———

2. Shift from local thinking to global thinking. God is a global God. He has always cared about the entire world.

Jesus said, "God so loved the world, that he gave his only begotten Son, that whosoever believeth in him should not perish, but have everlasting life."

JOHN 3:16 KJV

From one person God made all nations who live on earth, and he decided when and where every nation would be. God has done all this, so that we will look for him and reach out and find him.

ACTS 17:26–27 CEV

This same Good News that came to you is going out all over the world. It is changing lives everywhere, just as it changed yours.

COLOSSIANS 1:6 NLT

Jesus said, "You will tell everyone about me in Jerusalem, in all Judea, in Samaria, and everywhere in the world."

ACTS 1:8 CEV

In heaven an enormous crowd of people from "every race, tribe, nation, and language" will one day stand before Jesus Christ to worship him (Revelation 7:9 CEV).

Prayer is the most important tool for your mission in the world. What should you pray for?

Pray for opportunities to witness.

Pray for us . . . that God may open a door for our message, so that we may proclaim the mystery of Christ.

COLOSSIANS 4:3 NIV

———

"If you ask me, I will give you the nations;
   all the people on earth will be yours,"
      says the Lord.

PSALM 2:8 NCV

———

Pray for courage to speak up.

Don't forget to pray for me. Pray that I'll know what to say and have the courage to say it at the right time, telling the mystery to one and all, the Message that I . . . am responsible for getting out.

EPHESIANS 6:19–20 THE MESSAGE

———

Pray for those who will believe.

Jesus prayed, "My prayer is not for [my disciples] alone. I pray also for those who will believe in me through their message, that all of them may be one, Father, just as you are in me and I am in you."

JOHN 17:20–21 NIV

Pray for the rapid spread of the message.

Pray for us that the message of the Lord may spread rapidly and be honored, just as it was with you.

2 THESSALONIANS 3:1 NIV

Pray for more workers.

Jesus said to his disciples, "The harvest is plentiful but the workers are few. Ask the Lord of the harvest, therefore, to send out workers into his harvest field."

MATTHEW 9:37–38 NIV

Prayer makes you a partner with others around the world. Pray for missionaries and everyone else involved in the global harvest.

You are also joining to help us when you pray for us.

2 CORINTHIANS 1:11 GWT

---

3. Shift from "here and now" thinking to eternal thinking.

We fix our eyes not on what is seen, but on what is unseen. For what is seen is temporary, but what is unseen is eternal.

2 CORINTHIANS 4:18 NIV

———

Jesus said, "Anyone who lets himself be distracted from the work I plan for him is not fit for the Kingdom of God."

LUKE 9:62 LB

———

Deal as sparingly as possible with the things the world thrusts on you. This world as you see it is on its way out.

1 CORINTHIANS 7:31 THE MESSAGE

———

Let us strip off anything that slows us down or holds us back.

HEBREWS 12:1 LB

———

Jesus said, "I tell you, use worldly wealth to gain friends for yourselves, so that when it is gone, you will be welcomed into eternal dwellings."

MATTHEW 6:20–21 CEV

———

By [being generous and doing good to others]
[the wealthy in this world] will be storing up real
treasure for themselves in heaven—it is the only
safe investment for eternity! And they will be
living a fruitful Christian life down here as well.

1 Timothy 6:9 LB

———

*4. Shift from thinking of excuses to thinking of
creative ways to fulfill your commission.*

When Jeremiah claimed he was too young to be a
prophet, God rejected his excuse,
    "Don't say that," the Lord replied, "for you
must go wherever I send you and say whatever I
tell you. And don't be afraid of the people, for I
will be with you and take care of you."

Jeremiah 1:7–8 NLT

———

**The Great Commission is your commission,
and doing your part is the secret to living a
life of significance.**

Jesus said, "Only those who throw away their
lives for my sake and for the sake of the Good
News will ever know what it means to really live!"

Mark 8:35 LB

———

REFLECTIONS

Balancing Your Life

Live life with a due sense of responsibility, not as those who do not know the meaning of life but as those who do.

EPHESIANS 5:15 PH.

Don't let the errors of evil people lead you down the wrong path and make you lose your balance.

1 PETER 3:17 CEV

Blessed are the balanced; they shall outlast everyone. Your life is a pentathlon of five purposes, which you must keep in balance.

They are summarized in two verses:

The Great Commandment

Jesus said, "'Love the Lord your God with all your heart and with all your soul and with all your mind.' This is the first and greatest commandment. And the second is like it: 'Love your neighbor as yourself.'"

MATTHEW 22:37–39 NIV

The Great Commission

Jesus said, "All authority in heaven and on earth has been given to me. Therefore go and make disciples of all nations, baptizing them in the name of the Father and of the Son and of the Holy Spirit, and teaching them to obey everything I have commanded you. And surely I am with you always, to the very end of the age."

MATTHEW 28:18–20 NIV

These two statements of Jesus sum up God's five purposes for your life:

"Love God with all your heart": You were planned for God's pleasure, so your purpose is to love God through *worship*.

———

"Love your neighbor as yourself": You were shaped for serving, so your purpose is to show love for others through *ministry*.

———

"Go and make disciples": You were made for a mission, so your purpose is to share God's message through *evangelism*.

———

"baptize them into. . . ": You were formed for God's family, so your purpose is to identify with his church through *fellowship*.

———

"teach them to do all things. . . ": You were created to become like Christ, so your purpose is to grow to maturity through *discipleship*.

———

Keeping these five purposes in balance is not easy. But you can keep your life balanced and on track by developing these habits.—

1. Talk it through with a spiritual partner or small group.

As iron sharpens iron,
    so people can improve each other.
                    PROVERBS 27:17 NCV

———

Encourage each other and give each other strength.
                    1 THESSALONIANS 5:11 NCV

———

Put into practice what you have learned.
                    PHILIPPIANS 4:9 TEV

———

2. *Give yourself a regular spiritual check-up.*

Let us test and examine our ways.
Let us turn again in repentance to the Lord.

LAMENTATIONS 3:40 NLT

———

Each one should test his own actions. Then he can take pride in himself, without comparing himself to somebody else.

GALATIANS 6:4 NIV

———

Test yourselves to make sure you are solid in the faith. Don't drift along taking everything for granted. Give yourselves regular checkups. You need firsthand evidence, not mere hearsay, the Jesus Christ is in you. Test it out. If you fail the test, do something about it.

2 CORINTHIANS 13:5 THE MESSAGE

———

Let's take a good look at the way we're living and reorder our lives under God.

LAMENTATIONS 3:40 THE MESSAGE

———

Let your enthusiastic idea at the start be equaled by your realistic action now.

2 CORINTHIANS 8:11 LB

———

3. Write down your spiritual progress in a journal.

It's crucial that we keep a firm grip on what we've heard so that we don't drift off.

HEBREWS 2:1 THE MESSAGE

————

At the LORD's direction, Moses kept a written record of [the Israelites'] progress.

NUMBERS 33:2 NLT

————

Moses recorded the stages in [the Israelites'] journey.

NUMBERS 33:2 NIV

————

Write down for the coming generation what the
    LORD has done,
  so that people not yet born will praise him.

PSALM 102:18 TEV

————

4. *Pass on what you know to others.*

The one who blesses others is abundantly
   blessed;
      those who help others are helped.

PROVERBS 11:25 THE MESSAGE

———

I want you to tell [the things you've learned] to
followers who can be trusted to tell others.

2 TIMOTHY 2:2 CEV

———

Anyone who knows the right thing to do, but does
not do it, is sinning.

JAMES 4:17 NCV

———

If you teach [what you've learned] to other
followers, you will be a good servant of Christ
Jesus.

1 TIMOTHY 4:6 CEV

———

**The reason we pass on what we learn is for
the glory of God and the growth of his
kingdom.**

Jesus prayed, "I have brought you glory on earth,
Father, by completing the work you gave me to
do."

JOHN 17:4 NIV

———

REFLECTIONS

_____

_____

_____

_____

_____

_____

_____

_____

_____

_____

_____

_____

_____

_____

_____

_____

_____

_____

Living With Purpose

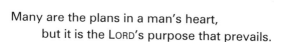

Many are the plans in a man's heart,
   but it is the Lord's purpose that prevails.
PROVERBS 19:21 NIV

Many are the plans in a man's heart,
David . . . served the purpose of God in his own
generation.

ACTS 13:36 NASB

Living on purpose is the only way to *really* live. Everything else is just existing. Unfortunately, it's easy to get distracted and forget what is most important. To prevent this, you should develop a purpose statement for your life and review it regularly.

Jesus said, "Now that you know [the things I've taught you], you will be blessed if you do them."
JOHN 13:17 NIV

What is a Life Purpose Statement?

1. It's a statement that summarizes God's purposes for your life.

God's plans endure forever;
  his purposes last eternally.

PSALM 33:11 TEV

Our purpose is to please God, not people.
1 THESSALONIANS 2:4 NLT

---

2. It's a statement that points the direction of your life.

Know where you are headed,
    and you will stay on solid ground.

PROVERBS 4:26 CEV

———

An intelligent person aims at wise action,
    but a fool starts off in many directions.

PROVERBS 17:24 TEV

———

3. It's a statement that defines "success" for you.

I want you to understand what really matters.
PHILIPPIANS 1:10 NLT

———

4. It's a statement that clarifies your roles.

You will have different roles at different stages in life, but your purposes will never change.

5. It's a statement that expresses your shape.

It reflects the unique ways God made you to serve him.

Here are five questions you should consider as you prepare your Life Purpose Statement:

1. Worship: What will be the center of my life?

[King Asa told the people of Judah to] center their lives on God.

2 CHRONICLES 14:4 THE MESSAGE

I pray that Christ will be more and more at home in your hearts.

EPHESIANS 3:17

A sense of God's wholeness, everything coming together for good, will come and settle you down. It's wonderful what happens when Christ displaces worry at the center of your life.

PHILIPPIANS 4:7 THE MESSAGE

2. Discipleship: What will be the character of my life?

Don't lose a minute in building on what you've been given, complementing your basic faith with good character, spiritual understanding, alert discipline, passionate patience, reverent wonder, warm friendliness, and generous love.

2 PETER 1:5 THE MESSAGE

―

Keep a firm grasp on both your character and your teaching. Don't be diverted. Just keep at it.

1 TIMOTHY 4:16 THE MESSAGE

―

3. *Ministry: What will be the contribution of my life?*

This service you perform not only meets the needs of God's people, but also produces an outpouring of gratitude to God.

2 CORINTHIANS 9:12 TEV

———

Jesus said, "I commissioned you to go out and to bear fruit, fruit that will last."

JOHN 15:16 NJB

———

4. Mission: What will be the communication *of my life?*

As for me and my family, we will serve the LORD.

JOSHUA 24:15 NLT

―――

Be sure that you live in a way that brings honor to the Good News of Christ.

PHILIPPIANS 1:27 NCV

―――

5. Fellowship: What will be the community *of my life?*

Christ loved the church and gave his life for it.
 EPHESIANS 5:25 TEV

The more you mature, the more you will love the Body of Christ and want to sacrifice for it, just as Jesus did.

In addition to writing a detailed life purpose statement, it is also helpful to have a shorter statement or slogan that summarizes the five purposes of your life in a way that's *memorable* and *inspires* you.

It will be good to keep these things in mind
so that you are ready to repeat them.
PROVERBS 22:18 NCV

———

God wants to use you. Will you serve God's purpose in *your* generation?

Our goal is to measure up to God's plan for us.
2 CORINTHIANS 10:13 LB

———

David . . . served God's purpose in his own generation.
ACTS 13:36 NIV

———

The eyes of the LORD search the whole earth in order to strengthen those whose hearts are fully committed to him.
2 CHRONICLES 16:9 NLT

———

I run straight to the goal with purpose in every step.
1 CORINTHIANS 9:26 NLT

———

Like Esther, God created you "for such a time as this" (Esther 4:14).

When fulfilling your purposes seems tough, don't give in to discouragement. Remember your reward, which will last forever.

Our light and momentary troubles are achieving for us an eternal glory that far outweighs them all.

2 CORINTHIANS 4:17 NIV

Imagine standing before the throne of God presenting our lives in deep gratitude and praise to Christ. Together we will say,

Worthy, Oh Master! Yes, our God! Take the glory! the honor! the power! You created it all; It was created because you wanted it!

REVELATION 4:11 THE MESSAGE

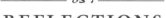

REFLECTIONS

_____

_____

_____

_____

_____

_____

_____

_____

_____

_____

_____

_____

_____

_____

_____

_____

_____

_____

_____

_____

Why Use So Many Translations?

I have intentionally varied the Bible translations used in this book for two important reasons. First, no matter how wonderful a translation is, it has limitations. The Bible was originally written using 11,280 Hebrew, Aramaic, and Greek words, but the typical English translation uses only around 6,000 words. Obviously, nuances and shades of meaning can be missed, so it is always helpful to compare translations.

Second, and even more important, is the fact that we often miss the full impact of familiar Bible verses, not because of poor translating, but simply because they have become so familiar! Therefore I have deliberately used paraphrases in order to help you see God's truth in new, fresh ways.

RICK WARREN

Sources

At Inspirio we love to hear from you—your

stories, your feedback,
and your product ideas.
Please send your comments to us
by way of e-mail at
icares@zondervan.com
or to the address below:

inspirio™

Attn: Inspirio Cares
5300 Patterson Avenue SE
Grand Rapids, MI 49530

If you would like further information
about Inspirio and the products we
create please visit us at:
www.inspiriogifts.com

Thank you and God Bless!